# DAUGHTERS AT SCHOOL

INSTRUCTED

IN A SERIES OF LETTERS.

BY THE REV. RUFUS W. BAILEY.

PHILADELPHIA:
PRESBYTERIAN BOARD OF PUBLICATION,
NO. 821 CHESTNUT STREET.

*STEREOTYPED BY*
JESPER HARDING & SON,
NO. 57 SOUTH THIRD STREET, PHILADELPHIA.

## ADVERTISEMENT.

THE following Letters are collected and published nearly as they were originally written. They originated in a desire to meet the expressed will of a dying mother that two daughters of tender age should be educated for eternity. In all other respects, they explain themselves.

# CONTENTS.

# DAUGHTERS AT SCHOOL.

## LETTER I.

### EDUCATION FOR ETERNITY.

My dear Children:—The deep solicitude which agitates the bosom of a parent is equalled only by the responsibilities which this relation imposes. In the early removal of your dear mother to a better world, this solicitude and these responsibilities press upon me with two-fold power. Although you can never realize them, nor appreciate the feelings by which my heart is deeply moved, I am often gratified to perceive, that the lapse of several years has not effaced your filial recollections of your departed parent, nor weakened the force of those peculiar and hallowed associations, by the aid of which a living parent attempts to enforce upon you her lessons of wisdom. It is with a desire to keep alive these associations, and to fulfil her expressed wishes, that I now propose to address to you a series of letters, prepared in my intervals of professional duties, and commended to your prayerful and serious consideration, as the sacred and disinterested expressions of a parent's full heart.

I need not urge assiduous application to your present duties. The expense at which I am furnishing you with the literary advantages of the most approved boarding school; the limited period of time which the brevity of youth, the proper season for improvement, allows to these pursuits; and the desire, as well as necessity, of returning again soon to the bosom of your surviving parent, all demand of you diligence in your studies. With the Reports received from your teachers, and my own knowledge of your progress, I have generally expressed to you my satisfaction. But I wish you always to be deeply impressed with the great and important truth, that this is but a small part of your education.

Education! how much is implied in that comprehensive word, often so loosely employed! Confined even to a limited and literary course, it involves great responsibilities. But the education of an immortal soul for eternal life, how inconceivably solemn and momentous!

Your parents received you, my children, from the hand of God to be educated for him, and for eternity. They dedicated you to God in their hearts and by prayer, the first hour of your existence. As soon as you were of suitable age to be carried to the house of God, both your parents presented you to the Lord in the sacramental form employed in our church, and suited to secure covenant blessings to our children. You were baptized in the name of the Father, and of the Son, and of the Holy Ghost. Never shall I forget the solemnity and pious devotion with which your dear mother performed this part of her duty, nor the fervour and apparent faith with which she often pleaded the covenant promises of God on your behalf to the latest hour of her life. Imperfectly, indeed, but truly, your parents have sought to give you a religious education. We shall meet you after a brief existence here,—how brief, we are admonished by the sudden and early death of your most excellent mother,—we shall meet where she now is, in eternity.

I desire, therefore, to conduct your education for eternity. In all the separate parts of it, consider that *you are under a course of education for eternity.* Ask yourselves in every step of your progress, and in every branch of your studies or amusements, your labours or relaxations—"What bearing and influence is this to have on my eternal interests?" Ask yourselves, "What will my mother, now in heaven, think of this? Let me not grieve her pious soul, if she is permitted, as many suppose, to behold and know what is done on earth." Let a still higher motive even be brought to bear on your actions—*the presence of God*, from which you can never escape. Ask yourselves—"How will *God* approve of this?" and do nothing which will not stand that test. I know some think this will make us very gloomy, and spoil our joys, and weaken our energies. The opposite will be the fact. Sir Isaac Newton, Sir Matthew Hale, Mrs. Hannah More, and thousands of others among the most distinguished, and truly the greatest and most happy of our race, have gone through life in this way.

Your education here is for eternity. This is not subject to our choice. We cannot alter the fact. Your education must be for eternity. You soon lose all your relations to this world, and retain for ever the peculiar relations, for which your character at death is found fitted. This character is formed in time. You are now forming it. Your education makes it. It is impossible, then, to elude the conclusion that you are under a course of education for eternity. Be satisfied with nothing, then, in your conduct, employments or feelings, the eternal consequences of which you are afraid to meet.

If you will admit this great truth to its proper and uninterrupted influence on all your decisions and actions, that you are immortal beings; if you will think of this in every question of duty, I have no doubt I shall gain your cordial assent to all the important views I now propose to offer to you—and what is of still more consequence, I shall secure your practical adoption of them. But this you will find to be a most difficult effort. Youth and its sanguine anticipations, the world and its pleasures, untried fields of promise and expectation are all to be contradicted, and the lessons of wisdom are to be substituted for the dictates of passions that are strong, and desires that are ardent, and glowing hope and anticipation. When I tell you that youth is brief, and the pleasures of the world deceitful, and the promise which speaks to young imagination is false, I agree with myself, but perhaps shall contradict you. Shall I be heard? If that great truth can obtain a complete dominion in your minds, that you now *act for eternity*, and if I can also make you feel that you must shortly die, then I shall be heard, and this effort, which has a single regard to your welfare, will be crowned with success. In my exertions to educate you for eternity, you will receive a blessing, and we may all be prepared to meet and rejoice with your dear mother in a sinless world.

## LETTER II.

### NECESSITY OF PERSONAL RELIGION.

My dear Children,—Personal religion lies at the foundation of every preparation for usefulness or happiness, either in time or in eternity. It consists in a right state of feeling toward God, and consequently leads to a right course of acting under his government. With this simple definition, is it not perfectly plain that you can never, under the divine government, be happy without religion? Any happiness which you may be able to filch from forbidden sources, must be enjoyed under forgetfulness of God, and a temporary unconsciousness of his all-pervading presence. But this forgetfulness will soon give place to the action of a quick memory of the past, and a conscious presence of God, from which the soul can never retire. "Acquaint thyself, therefore, now with God, and be at peace."

One objection to an early attention to religion, and only one, I will notice—as with many it operates more than all others to suspend attention to it—"It spoils our joys." My dear children, I, who give you such proofs of a deep interest in your happiness, can I be suspected of a design to spoil your joys, to abridge your happiness? I shall not be so suspected. I tell you, then, that the contrary is the fact. Will you believe me? I refer you to facts. The most pious persons you have known or read of,—has their religion made them unhappy? Has it not manifestly, and by their own testimony, been the source of their principal happiness? And is not this a sufficient answer to the assertion, or suspicion, that "religion spoils our joys?" I refer you, finally, to your recollections of your dear mother. She mingled but little with the world. But was she not happy? She was cheerful in society, not gay—but always most happy when engaged in religious conversation, reading or devotion. Her religious character commenced in early life, and if you would imitate her example, you must not delay to give attention to your own personal religion. It will not spoil your joys. It will increase them by opening larger and more permanent sources of happiness. I would rather hear that you have become religious, than to hear that you are counted among the first scholars in the school, and have taken the first honours in your classes. Yes, my dear children, dearer to me than any other possession, I would rather hear that you have died with a "good hope in Christ," than to hear that you are growing up in every useful attainment and mental endowment, but hardening in sin, and living "without hope and without God in the world."

Your dear departed mother has been heard speaking once on this subject from the borders of eternity; her voice now comes from the instructive grave. Her last three letters written to you I happen to have, preserved from many, which have been carelessly destroyed. She died on the 11th of November, 1832. These letters were written at intervals of about five, two, and one month, previous to her decease. The first is dated June 18, as follows:—

"My dear Children,—Your mother has not forgotten you, although she has so long delayed to answer your letters. Not a day passes but she thinks often and affectionately of her little daughters, and prays that the precious privileges they enjoy of improving their minds and hearts, may not pass unemployed. Remember, my dear girls, that youth is the most favourable time for storing the mind with useful knowledge, and that it is especially the season in which God, your heavenly father, has promised to be found of those who seek him—'They that seek me early shall find me.' I rejoice to hear that the Lord is in C——, by his Holy Spirit, waiting to be gracious to sinners, and that many have come to him for that new heart, without which none of us can enter into heaven, that holy, happy place, where the Lord Jesus, that dear friend of sinners, reigns in all his glory, and where sin, or pain, or death, can never enter. My dear children, remember you were born with sinful natures, that you cannot do one action that is not tainted with sin, that you cannot even think a good thought without the help of the Holy Spirit, that the Bible, which is the eternal truth, declares that except ye be converted, or born again, you cannot enter into the kingdom of heaven; and that now is the accepted time, and the day of salvation to all who are willing to forsake their sins and come to Christ. Soon this short life will be over with us all; with some very, very soon. Perhaps the next hour or next week may be our last on earth, and if you die without a new heart, you are lost—lost for ever! There are no pardons offered in the grave. No Saviour there stands pleading for sinners.

'But darkness, death, and long despair,
Reign in eternal silence there.'

"Oh think of these things, think of them daily, think of them seriously, and pray to God to impress them deeply upon your hearts, that you may not forget them amidst the allurements and temptations of this world. Do you want to make your dear parents happy? Do you want to enjoy peace which passeth understanding, in this world, and to be prepared to die with a song of praise upon your lips? and above all, do you want to show your love and gratitude to Him who left his throne, and robe of dazzling glory, and came into this world to die for his enemies? Do you want to be made like him, and to dwell with him for ever in his 'Father's house,' where are 'many mansions?' Oh, then, come to Jesus, now, in the morning of life. Give him your hearts. Commit your immortal souls into his hands to sanctify and redeem from sin, and you will find him faithful to perform his promise, and ready and able to save you from all your sins and fears, and to do abundantly more and better for you than you can ask or think. And you will fill the hearts of your affectionate, anxious parents with joy and gratitude, beyond what they can ever express.

"My dear children, such is my anxiety for your eternal salvation, and such my earnest desire that you may now hear the Saviour's voice, that I cannot refrain from writing in this urgent, importunate manner. Oh, do not disregard a tender mother's earnest entreaties. Do not read this letter once in a careless, thoughtless manner, and think no more about it. But read it with prayer to God to sanctify it to you. Read it as you would, if it were the last dying message of your dear mother—as if it were the last call you would ever have to repentance and life—and may God, who is rich in mercy to all who call upon his name, hear your earnest, fervent prayers for grace, and give you his Holy Spirit to sanctify and lead you into all truth.

"When you write again, let me know if you want anything for your comfort, and especially let me know whether you do resolve to seek the Lord Jesus for your friend. Let me hear a good report of you in all things. 'Study to be quiet and to mind your own business.' Be affectionate and kind to all your companions, and especially in your intercourse as sisters.

'Let love through all your actions run,
Let all your words be mild,
Live like the blessed Virgin's son,
That sweet and lovely child.'"

Such is the letter which I now ask you to re-peruse, treasure up, and carefully meditate upon, as the dying instructions of your much loved mother—and what they could not then avail in arresting your attention, and compelling your choice, may I not hope they will now do, when she speaks as from the grave, and when maturer years commend these lessons to your riper judgment and experience?

## LETTER III.

### PERSONAL RELIGION.

My dear Children,—The second letter of your dear mother to which I have alluded, and now in my possession, is dated September 2nd. The judicious and comprehensive instructions respecting your studies, contained in several of the first sentences, are a specimen of her matured and excellent views on education; but it is to the religious thoughts urged upon you that I wish to direct your attention. The letter is as follows:—

"My dear Children,— Your letters have given me much satisfaction. I am glad to see the improvement in your hand-writing, and hope you make good progress in all your studies. Your last Reports speak very well of your recitations. You must try to understand perfectly all you undertake to learn, or it will do you very little good. I approve, Mary, of your studying Geography and History, rather than Mineralogy, at your present age. I wish you to obtain a thorough knowledge of Modern and Ancient Geography,

History, and English Grammar, and be able to apply with readiness any of the rules of Arithmetic to the practical purposes of life, and then you can more profitably attend to other branches. Do not neglect your hand-writing, but try to write every line better than the last, and after you have formed a habit of writing with care, you will soon write with ease, as well as elegance.

"My dear children, I need not tell you how much or often my thoughts dwell upon you, or how many anxieties fill my heart lest you suffer the precious morning of life to pass away, without forming your minds and heart to those habits of virtue and piety, which alone can secure your usefulness and happiness, as you pass through the many changes and trials of this life, or secure your safety and felicity in that world where changes are unknown. Think often of your relations to God. He is your heavenly Father, from whom you have received life, and all the blessings you enjoy—and can you forget daily and hourly to thank him, and to show your gratitude by doing what he requires of you?

"Ask yourselves very often—For what was I placed in this world? Surely this is not the place where you will live for ever. Your friends and acquaintances are dying constantly about you, and their bodies are laid in the silent tomb, where there is 'no knowledge, or wisdom, or device.' Their work is done, and their account sealed up to the judgment day, when they will be called to give an account of all the deeds done in the body, and receive a reward according to their works. Those who have done the will of God by believing on the Lord Jesus Christ, and following him through this world of sin, will receive a crown of glory that fadeth not. But those who have hardened their hearts, and not listened to, nor obeyed the gospel, where, oh where will they appear? It will then be too late to pray for mercy. Jesus, the once kind and interceding Saviour, will then be their angry Judge. They must 'go away into everlasting punishment.'

"Apply these things to yourselves, and think—Must I, too, soon die? Must I give an account to God for all my words, thoughts, and actions? Is Jesus, the kind Saviour of sinners, now speaking to me in his gospel, to look unto him and be saved? And shall I not look and live for ever? Shall I not give him the morning, the best of my days, and all, perhaps, that I shall have to give, when he laid down his life for such sinners as I am? And that, too, when this is not only the path of safety, but the only path of happiness?

"Oh, my children, think of these things, and lift up your hearts to God in prayer, that he may teach you, and impart to you that living faith, which will enable you to understand and receive the gospel. If God is pleased to spare your lives, your parents will not long be here to care for, or instruct you. They too must die, and you know not how soon. Oh, let them see their children walking in the truth, and they will die in peace.

"I did not think of saying so much on this subject when I began this letter, but when I think of the worth of your souls, and the danger of your dying without securing your salvation, I feel that I cannot refrain from urging you to attend to these things without delay. Listen, my children, to the advice of a mother, as perhaps the last she will ever give. I wish you both to write soon after receiving this, and let me know what you want, and what are your thoughts and feelings upon that subject which occupies so much of your parents' anxious thoughts.

## LETTER IV.

### EARLY PIETY.

My dear Children,—The last letter of your dear mother, written to you about a month before her death, I now commend to your serious re-perusal.

"My dear Children,—I have been lately engaged in preparing the white dresses, which I send with this, and which you should have had earlier, but for the want of leisure to get them ready. You are old enough now to attend to your own clothes, and see that everything is in order, and in its proper place, and I hope you will feel a pleasure in doing it, and also in assisting each other to do the same. You can do much towards each other's improvement, as well as comfort. Be attentive and kind to each other at all times, and try to be thankful, that in possessing a sister, you each have a blessing that is denied to many. Let no unkind word pass between you, or envious feeling be harboured in your hearts, but conduct towards each other, every day, as you would if you believed it to be the last day you would live together; and then, should it please your heavenly Father to separate you, you will have no bitter reflections in reviewing your former inter course, but will be prepared to meet again in peace and love in a better world.

"I was very much pleased with the letters you sent by Mrs. M——, both with the improvement in your hand-writing, and also with the evidence that the subject upon which I last wrote you, and which, of all others, is the most important, had not passed entirely from your minds, but that you felt disposed to make inquiries, and to apply the truth to yourselves.

"You say, my dear Mary, you 'do not fully understand the subject of conversion, and cannot feel that you are a greater sinner than any one else.' But do you not feel, my dear child, that you have a disposition or heart inclined to evil thoughts, to forgetfulness of God, your best and kindest friend, and to the neglect of his holy word? And is it not very difficult to fix your mind and heart entirely upon God, when you attempt to pray to him? And are you not more ready to believe what the world and the wicked father of lies say, than what your Creator says, who loves you infinitely better than your earthly parents, or any earthly friend can? Ask yourself these and the like questions, praying to God to

3

enlighten and teach you, and you will soon discover that your heart is by nature alienated from God, without true and holy love to him, and that, if you were to go to heaven with such feelings, where the whole employment is to praise and serve a holy God who hates sin, you could not be happy there. And then you will see how necessary it is that these evil inclinations should be subdued, and that you have a new heart given you, a heart which can love God supremely, because he hates sin, and is infinitely worthy to be loved, and which can hate and avoid sin, because it is opposed to such a holy God.

"I do not think, my dear, it is required of you to feel that you have committed more sinful actions than any others, for it is very true that you have not as many as thousands. But the evil is, you have just such a heart by nature as the most hardened sinner had, and if it should please God to leave you entirely to yourself to follow these evil inclinations, you would soon commit the same crimes and come to the same miserable end. Thus you see, it is not because you are by nature better than the greatest sinner, but because God has been pleased to keep you from temptations, to which others have been exposed. And let me assure you, my dear children, that if you sincerely look to him by humble prayer, he will ever thus keep you from the sins that are in the world.

He will give you a right heart and put a right spirit within you, that you may be able to keep all his commandments, and rely on a Saviour's righteousness for salvation.

"It is my anxious desire and daily prayer that you may understand this great subject, and early come to Christ, and learn of Him to be meek and humble christians, and then you will know what conversion means, and enjoy that peace which all the riches or honours of this world can never give, and which all adverse or trying scenes cannot take away. I hope you both remember and read your precious Bibles every day—not as a task, but to understand what God says to you, for this is the only book in which you can learn his will. And here he plainly says, 'They that seek me early, shall find me.' I can say no more at present, but commit you to the kind care of Him who is able to keep you from all evil, and to present you faultless before his throne of glory."

Thus your dear mother closed her instructions to you, committing you to "Him who is able to keep you from evil." This she did frequently with fervency, and I trust with faith. She sunk into the grave rapidly, in an illness of ten days. She once only expressed a desire to live—it was for you, not for herself. Her care for you in the smallest matters is exhibited in these letters; but the ruling desire of her heart stands out in bold relief—that you may be born again, as the children of God. I have copied some paragraphs which relate to smaller matters, that you may be influenced by them as the instructions of your dying mother, on several practical subjects of secondary, but great importance. It is to the most comprehensive and complete exhibition of the great interest of the soul, given by her in a few paragraphs, I shall call your attention, and endeavour only to enforce what she has, in the best manner, said.

## LETTER V.

### EARLY PIETY.

My dear Children:—On the subject of conversion I ask your prayerful attention to the instructions contained in the last letters of your dear mother. They present you an admirable and comprehensive view of the theology of the subject in the utterly depraved and helpless condition of the soul, the necessity of regeneration by the Holy Ghost, the duty of immediate repentance and faith in Christ, and the encouragement to personal exertion on the ground of the provisions and promises extended in the word of God. Then, your duty is enforced upon you by a solemn reference to the uncertainty of life, since made more impressive by her own early and sudden decease; and finally her full soul is poured out in the expression of a burning desire that you would embrace the precious promises made to those who seek God early. I shall now only attempt to enforce the last appeal.

Is there great reward in keeping the commandments of God? Then the greatest reward is to those who keep them from their youth. Is the service of God, on the whole, to be preferred to the service of sin? then that service should be chosen at once. If youth sacrifices great enjoyments by renouncing the world, it avoids great temptations and hazards, and secures equally great religious pleasures. The ardour, and freshness, and vigour which give a zest to the pleasures of this world to the young, prepare them also for a higher field of pleasurable exercise in religious pursuits. Every argument which can be urged in favour of a religious life, applies to youth with not less appropriateness than to age; while some of the most important apply with much greater force, and others exclusively, to youth. By some of these arguments I shall urge the duty of early religion on my little daughters.

There is a special promise: "they that seek me early shall find me." Whatever various applications the term *early* may here admit of, there is no doubt it applies with peculiar emphasis to early life. It furnishes special encouragement to the young to seek the Lord. The Lord is well pleased with an early and prompt sacrifice. It is reasonable it should be so. By sin we provoke God to depart from us. He is, therefore, nearer to us in early life than when we have grown up in sin, so that there are really fewer difficulties in the way of a religious life in youth than in more advanced years. Every sin presents an additional difficulty in our approaches to God. All, who have carefully watched and observed the influence of sin, although their experience may be of limited duration, can testify to the truth of this remark. We come with less facility to ask a favour where we are conscious of having inflicted an injury. You know it is your duty to give your hearts, in all their affections, to God. Refusing to do this, you wrong your Benefactor, your Maker, as well as yourselves. This simple act of refusal diminishes your estimation of yourselves, and covers you with shame, and fills you with want of confidence in a consciousness of ill desert when you attempt to go again. Do you not feel less facility, as well as less inclination to pray, after you have omitted the stated duty, or been irregular in the performance of it? You do. Here is the illustration. The difficulties multiply in an increasing ratio, as these duties are successively neglected through successive periods of time. The farther we go from God, the deeper is the darkness which gathers upon our path, and the harder is it to retrace our steps. This is the united testimony of age, corroborated by your own brief experience. Hence the urgency of the duty to seek God early. Hence the propriety of the exhortation, and the truth of the promise. My children, will you not seek God early?

But there is a second argument by which I urge upon your notice this promise of God, now called to your acceptance by the exhortation of your dear mother—it is the uncertainty of life. How uncertain, you have been taught by painful experience, by the death of a sister much younger than yourselves, and more recently by the sudden decease of the watchful guardian of your earlier years, whose counsels and care were of the highest importance to you. These letters, which the loss of her maternal counsels alone has called forth, are to you a memento of the uncertainty of life. I believe either of you would shudder at the thought of dying, destitute of personal religion. Let that thought possess your minds under a full conviction of all the uncertainty of life, and I am sure there must be an awakening in your thoughtful minds, which will not easily be quieted. The certainty of death—and the uncertainty of life! Oh, how these truths press on the interests of the immortal soul! Think, my children! to die with no interest in the Saviour, to die young—to meet your departed mother beyond the grave, and we shall meet her; what is more, to meet God your Judge, having been thus urged to seek him early—to die young with no interest in the atoning blood of Christ, can you entertain the thought? and yet, can you deliberately dismiss it under such a pressure of motives to dwell upon it? To grow up in sin, and harden under the distinguished means of grace you enjoy, to risk all the difficulties of a deferred repentance, and then to think of the possibility of dying accursed in old age, can you endure the thought? Can you shield your hearts against the multiplied and pressing motives to immediate repentance? My dear children, think of the uncertainty of life, and then say, will you seek the Lord early while he may be found? Will you call upon him while he is near?

## LETTER VI.

### EARLY PIETY.

MY DEAR CHILDREN,—Simply to be religious neither fulfils our duty nor brings to us our full privilege. We ought to strive to be eminently good. This will make us eminently useful and eminently happy. There are many who make a religious profession, and who seem to give a general evidence that they are sincere. We cannot question their piety. And yet they have no zeal, and exert but little influence. There are others who are active and efficient, happy and joyful in their religion. I do not doubt you would desire to be classed with the latter.

This difference of character depends on two causes—the thoroughness of the work of grace on the heart, and the period of life at which that work is accomplished. The work of grace is God's, and in the specific act of regeneration we are the passive subjects of a divine efficiency, yet nothing is more obvious than the truth that the direction of our minds to religious subjects, and the degree of interest they gain, and influence they exert, depend, to a great extent, on the use or employment of powers over which we have a control, and for the employment of which, therefore, we shall be held responsible as moral agents. You can use the means of grace or neglect them. You can dismiss one train of thought and adopt another of an opposite character and influence. You can withdraw your attention from one set of objects and direct it to another. This mental discipline is your own, and is sufficient to show you that the work of grace on the heart may be invited, and entertained, or resisted by you—and also that its thoroughness depends very much on yourselves. If you "resist the Holy Ghost," you "grieve him away." If you seek him early, "he will be found."

Another reason for the difference which we see in christian character may be looked for in the period of life when that character is formed. Those who begin early have every advantage. They commence a course of discipline and learning in the school of Christ, before habits are formed which must be abandoned—sins indulged which must embitter every hour of future life—and while the young affections are ardent to embrace zealously, and identify themselves with, their object. Early christians make the best, the most eminent christians. They have their whole lives to grow in knowledge and in grace. There is one other consideration—God requires our best service. It is a high indignity we offer to him, when we withhold the first fruits, the best, and bring as an offering to him the maimed, the halt and the blind. My children, will you not give your early life, your youth, to the service of God?

Another argument may be drawn from a regard to your own personal happiness. Our religious joys depend on the reflections and convictions of our own minds. How elevated and pure must be that joy which attends a sense of duty faithfully, fearlessly, and always rendered! Conscience awards its approbation, and harmonizes with all the powers of the soul in a universal homage to the law. You can read your own history without a blush, and review the past with pleasure. You will, indeed, find subjects for humiliation and repentance, but an enlightened conscience has been regarded in the admonitions it gave, and the understanding, illuminated by the Holy Spirit, has been allowed to teach. Far different will be the reflections of mature years and of old age, if you now succeed in silencing the voice of the divine Teacher, and in shutting out the light he sheds upon the mind.

Shall I not add—your best and constant service is due to God? You owe him all. Do you intend to secure an interest in his love before you die? Do it now. Can you not bear the thought of dying his enemy? Do not, then, suffer yourselves to live his enemy for a single day. If he deserves your love, he deserves your early love. If he deserves your service, surely you ought not to be willing to offer him the precarious remnant of old age, decrepitude and sin. Come, then, without delay, and give yourselves to God. Dedicate yourselves in all you have, and all you are to him, and you will find, in the service of religion, pleasures which will more than compensate for all you leave when you "forsake the world."

In regard to the difficulties you may imagine or realize to obstruct your way, I have only to say—tell them all to God. There is an open throne of grace. Do you "not understand the subject of conversion?"—reverently express your ignorance to God and pray for light. Do you find darkness and difficulties in the way? Lay them all before your heavenly Father, and pray for their removal. The pious women who went to the sepulchre on the morning of the resurrection, inquired of one another as they went, "Who shall roll us away the stone from the door of the sepulchre?" But when they arrived, they found the stone rolled away, and their faith was confirmed. Just so it often is with sinners, who expect great and insuperable difficulties to obstruct their way. These difficulties often give way, or are entirely removed as they proceed, while those who have been discouraged by the prospect of them, continue and die in their sins. Instead of complaining and suffering discouragement—pray. Go forward—it is your life.

My dear children, I solemnly admonish you to lay at the foundation of your education the cultivation of personal religion. Eternity! do you comprehend it? As much as its duration exceeds the measure of a day, does the importance of religion exceed every other object of personal effort or attainment. Remember, always, that your education is for eternity, and "whatsoever a man soweth that shall he also reap. He that soweth to the flesh, shall of the flesh reap corruption—but he that soweth to the Spirit, shall of the Spirit reap life everlasting." Youth is the seed time of what we shall reap in old age, and time ripens the fruit which we gather, in eternity.

## LETTER VII.

### A SINNER WITHOUT HOPE.

My dear Harriet,—Two letters received within a few days from your dear sister, have filled my heart with inexpressible joy. They inform me that a revival of religion has commenced in your school, that many young ladies are anxiously inquiring what they shall do to be saved, that several have already obtained a hope of pardon, and that she humbly places her own name with the latter class. But in the midst of my joy for one child saved, how does my mind hurry back, under the deep impulse of parental anxiety, to inquire for the other left in ruin! My dear Harriet, how is it with you? The silence observed towards my last note asking this question, is portentous, and full of expressiveness. If you felt an evidence of pardon and acceptance with God, you would be ready to speak for your Saviour. I receive your silence as a sad negation to my ardent desires, my fervent prayers and cherished hopes—you have no hope!

In this simple attitude then, I propose now to

address you. Dear and cherished in the natural affection and sympathy of a father, spared as a monument of divine forbearance, called to repentance by the ministry, the word, and the Spirit of God—you are still a sinner, an unpardoned, condemned sinner.

I shall attempt to fix your attention on a few plain, but important and fundamental truths, which I ask you seriously to examine, and then give me the result of your deliberate thoughts.

You live under a government of laws. To understand your case then, you have only to consider the nature and extent of the divine law, and what you have done under that law.

The law of God is the eternal rule of right, which depends on his own nature, and which he applies to regulate the conduct of his creatures. As it depends upon, and grows out of, his nature, it exhibits his moral character and perfections; and we love God when we love his law, and hate God when we feel an enmity to the strictness and purity of his law. Obedience to the law, therefore, is always the best evidence of love to God, and disobedience is a proof of enmity. This law is summarily comprehended in the Ten Commandments. The first four of these are called the first table, and relate to the duties we owe to God. The last six are called the second table, and comprise our duties to our fellow men. These commandments were originally given in their present form with much ceremony to the children of Israel at Sinai, and written by Moses on two tables or tablets of stone. An epitome of these two tables was given by our Saviour in two sentences: "Thou shalt love the Lord thy God with all thy heart, and with all thy mind." "And thou shalt love thy neighbour as thyself." The first table requires the exercise of love to God; and the second table, the exercise of love to man. In his sermon on the mount, and at other times, the Saviour explains and applies this law as not only embracing our actions, but as reaching to all the thoughts and intents of the heart. God, omniscient and omnipresent, applies it thus strictly at all times, and in all places, throughout his moral universe.

The law of God, then, of which the sinner often entertains such vague notions, is very definite, readily comprehended even by a child, and easily applied. It regards the state of our hearts, and requires the exercise of love, pure, fervent and uninterrupted love to God and his creatures. Here our attention is withdrawn from all those perplexities which embarrass us in some of its mysteries, and also in every attempt to make out a balance sheet in a commercial debt and credit of good and bad deeds, according to our standard or the world's judgment of right and

4*

wrong. We are also relieved from the difficulties of that other plan of investigation, where we compare our characters with others for approbation or censure, as we may be better or worse than they are. The law of God is the standard; the state of heart is the action. The standard requires the exercise of positive love to God in the whole heart and soul and mind; in other words, in our whole intelligent and moral existence. The failure of this service is the action of the heart, which brings it into condemnation. This leads us directly to the subject matter of all the sinner's difficulty. You need not be troubled to decide the question whether you positively hate God. Do you positively love him? Do you approve of, admire and love that holy law, which condemns you as a sinner? Is it, in your estimation, "holy and just and good?"

It is a transcript of God's character, and when you love the law in its strict application to yourself, you love God. When you reject those applications of the law, or cannot sustain them, you hate God.

Here, then, you may easily see what kind of a sinner you have been. God says—"Give me thy heart." This you have withheld, and bestowed its affections on the creature. This is your sin. You need not say you have never murdered, nor lied, nor sworn profanely, nor stolen, nor coveted, nor worshipped idols. You have withheld from God your whole heart. Every moment you have done this, you have violated his law—you have incurred its penalty. Now, if you will count up the number of seconds you have lived since you were capable of understanding your duty, you will have the number of your actual sins in one particular, of one class only. All your other sins of every other kind are still to be added. O my child, what a sinner you have been! How can you answer for one of a thousand? May the Spirit of God teach you what a weight of guilt you carry with you to the judgment bar.

But to feel, to realize that you are a sinner—this is what you need. It is the nature of sin to harden the heart and pervert the understanding. Hence, sinners in the scriptures are called fools, because "having hearts," they act as if they "understood not." This effect of sin is often seen under the operation of human laws. A criminal arrested, charged with high crimes, and committed to prison, insensible to his guilt before arrest, often remains insensible and hardened. But let this criminal, charged with a capital offence against the laws, be brought out into open court; let him be arraigned, his crime defined and proved, and the law applied to the case; let judgment be solemnly pronounced upon him, the time and place of his execution appointed, and let him be remanded to his prison to await the sentence of the law. What then? It becomes real to him. He tries his native strength in vain to break through the walls which justice has built to hold him to the sentence of the law. He cannot force the massy bars by which he is held to answer for his crime. He is condemned. He knows it. He is left alone to feel that judgment has been passed upon him, and he awaits execution. Here it is very difficult for the sinner to stifle conviction, and remain insensible to his ruin.

This is precisely what you need to feel as a condemned sinner under the divine law. You are not in heaven, because not finally justified; not in hell, because not finally and irreversibly condemned. But you are on earth, a prisoner of hope; condemned and awaiting execution, but under a dispensation of mercy to see if you will not repent. What you need now is to feel, to realize precisely what the poor condemned criminal under law realizes when all hope of escape has fled for ever. You are in prison under sentence of death, temporal, spiritual and eternal death. You cannot escape. If you could leap the limits of this earth, you could not go beyond the universe of God, nor elude his observation, nor transcend the almighty power by which he holds you. This, my dear child, is what I desire you to feel. It is what we call conviction of sin.

## LETTER VIII.

### THE SINNER UNDER CONVICTION.

MY DEAR HARRIET,—Conviction of sin is effected in the heart by the special operations of the Holy Spirit. It is his work. He "reproves the world of sin, of righteousness, and of judgment." By the operation of a divine energy, he anticipates to the sinner's mind the judgment to come. This he does by producing in the mind, clear perceptions of the divine law in its nature and extent, by bringing to remembrance past sins in their multitude and enormity, and by applying the law to the case, so that his utter ruin and hopelessness under the regular operation of the divine government are clearly seen and realized. So lost is the sinner, that he is never fully sensible of his ruin, until the Spirit of God, by an almighty agency, brings him thus into judgment. Hence the value of those favoured seasons, when, as at Pentecost, this divine agency is exerted. Hence the privilege now enjoyed by you in a revival of religion, which this divine operation is carrying forward at B——. Oh, how important that you should cherish these heavenly and gracious influences! My dear child, are you convinced that you are a sinner? Then you need a Saviour. Are you such a sinner as I have described? Then you understand what kind of a Saviour you need. Do you ask, are you now awakened to the inquiry—"What shall I do to be saved?" Then I will lead your mind to another doctrine in the glorious plan of redemption.

To the sinner, condemned under the broken law of God, there is no hope of escape but in a dispensation of mercy. There is no help in himself, and if he cannot find, as under human laws, a pardoning power, he is utterly, hopelessly lost. But the law of God, being a transcript of his character, is necessarily *immutable*, and this is the law whose penalty has been incurred. What then can be done? Who can control this law? The immutable God cannot change it. Here you may be led to see what kind of a Saviour you need. And you can appreciate the value and necessity of a Mediator, who, in a divine nature, as "Daysman," may "lay his hand" upon the offended Lawmaker, and as Man, "lay his hand" upon the offending creatures, to treat for us, and bring us together; who, besides this, can make an atonement by which the law may be satisfied, and its penalty paid, and who may come in to accomplish this reconciliation, "not by destroying, but by fulfilling the law."

To the Son of God, then, the Eternal Word, the second person in the blessed Trinity, the attention of the convicted sinner is directed. As God Man, Mediator, he says, "Look unto me and be saved." "He bore our sins in his own body on the tree." "He is the end of the law for righteousness to every one that believeth." Now, then, it is declared, "He that *believeth* shall be saved, and he that believeth not shall be damned." "There is now no condemnation to them that are in Christ Jesus."

My dear child, here is a plan of redemption. It is a complete, glorious, safe plan. Are you a lost sinner? Christ "came to seek and to save them that were lost." Are you a sinner against an immutable law? The Maker of that law, in a "mystery," "has borne your sins in his own body on the tree." He has fulfilled that law. Are you a depraved sinner? "The blood of Jesus Christ cleanseth from all sin." "Who is he that condemneth? It is Christ that died, yea, rather, that is risen again, who is even at the right hand of God, who also maketh intercession for us." "It is God that justifieth."

Here is a glorious plan of redemption. It brings into the experience of the redeemed sinner an illustration of the glorious character of God in the doctrine of the blessed Trinity. It goes to the root of the evil of sin, and extirpates it.

It probes our wounds to the bottom, and heals them. It enters into the heart, the seat of our moral disease, and "cleanses it from all sin."

Do you still ask how you shall believe? I refer you again to the criminal in prison under sentence of death for the violation of a human law. Suppose you were that criminal thus condemned. Suppose your days were numbered and finished, and the sun had lighted up the last day of your gloomy confinement. Suppose while you were anxiously expecting the officers of justice to attend the last sad ceremonies of execution, your prison door should open to introduce to you a minister of religion, who, instead of the iron grasp of the executioner, should take your hand with a benignant smile, which assured you that he could feel for you and seek your welfare. He had obtained admittance in his official character as a minister of mercy. He tells you the gallows is erected, and the ministers of justice are at the door. There is but one hope for your life. Assume his apparel, and pass out in his name, and in his character, while he takes your place and averts the execution of the penalty from you. You might hesitate to save your own life, being guilty, by the substitution of an innocent sufferer. But he assures you that he will take care of that, and approve his plan to you when he shall himself come forth with life, and give you an opportunity to express your gratitude, and hail him as your benefactor. What would you do? Would not such love melt your heart? Would you find any difficulty in believing him, and regulating your action accordingly? Now here is a practical illustration. In your distress and exposure, let the love of Christ melt your heart. He enters your prison a messenger of mercy, and casts the robe of his own righteousness about you, and bids you go forth in his name and leave the rest to him. "*Believe*, and be saved." Now, cannot you *believe?* A lost sinner, and feeling your utter ruin and helplessness, and not see the beauty and strength there is in Christ! Not able to trust him as a Saviour! Then you must be lost. "There is no other name given under heaven whereby we must be saved." My dear child, come right to Christ, just as you are in your sins, and cast yourself on his mercy. Say, "God be merciful to me a sinner." "Lord, save me, or I perish." "Lord, I believe, help thou my unbelief." Do this, cherishing the same divine influences, by which you have been taught your danger and your helplessness, and then tell me the result.

## LETTER IX.

### THE SINNER UNDER CONVICTION.

MY DEAR HARRIET:—I regard your mind as awakened to a sense of your danger, when you say you "feel that you are a great sinner in the sight of God."

If you feel this, my dear child, I bless God—it is from him—it is not of yourself. It is the work of his Spirit. Sinners, in the power and pride of their own minds, speculate and theorize, they do not feel. You say you feel, realize, that you are a sinner. Here then is the application of the truth. It is the office of the Holy Spirit to "reprove, convince the world of sin." This the sinner never feels personally, except under the influence of this divine agency.

But you "feel that you are a great sinner"—you feel that you are a sinner and a great sinner. Surely, my child, this is of God. Sinners, by their own rule and their own light, are not disposed to regard themselves as great sinners, because they do not consider the spirituality and extent and strictness of the divine law, and its application especially to themselves. They compare themselves with themselves, and judge by rules they have formed or at least perverted, and always with great allowance in their own favour. Thus, like Saul of Tarsus, they are "alive without the law" or without the application of it. But when the "commandment comes," or is applied to themselves, they feel, like the same offender, now become a distinguished disciple, that they are "the chief of sinners." If you had committed but a single sin, and standing alone with no comparison of your guilt with others, if you judge yourself by the strictness of God's law, you must feel that you are a great sinner. This is what the Spirit of God invariably teaches, and no one, who has not felt this, has ever been taught of God, has ever yet taken the first step in christian experience.

But you say you feel also that you are a great sinner—"in the sight of God." Here is something of serious import—in the sight of God! The sinner commonly goes on in sin, not realizing that God sees him. He lives quietly in his guilt, because he shuts his eyes to his own sin, while he rolls it as a sweet morsel under his tongue, and it is in his mouth sweet as honey. But when the law is announced, and he understands it, he perceives the presence of God. He is present in that law, which is a transcript of his character. Then the sinner sees his own wickedness, not in comparison with other sinners, but in direct contrast with the character of God. Here he is a "sinner in the sight of God."

Are you a "sinner in the sight of God?" Do you mean to say that you have those views of the purity and holiness of the divine character and the divine law, which have bid you "feel that you are a great sinner in his sight?" Then, my dear child, God has spoken to you. Oh, listen while he speaks! Give your attention. Cherish, with the most lively anxiety, those divine illuminations. God from his throne speaks to you.

These seasons of special awakening are of great and eventful moment in the sinner's history. He is roused from his common lethargy and unconcern, and is brought into the presence of God—to see himself a sinner before God and his judge—to see the law of God, in all its strictness and justice, applied to his actual life. To recede from the convictions and calls of such divine illuminations, is to repel the counsels and threatenings of God distinctly heard, and to go away from his presence. Once slighted, these calls are rarely repeated with equal impressiveness; these lessons are seldom given again with equal power to arrest attention. Therefore, I say, cherish these divine influences, and yield to the strong convictions of the present favoured mediatorial hour.

The scripture direction given to a "great sinner in the sight of God," I employed in the instructions of my last letter. "Repent and believe in the Lord Jesus Christ." If you see yourself a sinner in the sight of God, you see what a loathsome object you are, as all sinners are, in his presence. You must then abhor yourself as Job did, when he saw God in the purity of his character; and you must repent, or be sorry for your sins, as in dust and ashes.

Are you in this low condition—a poor condemned and ruined sinner in the convictions of your own mind? Then how loathsome an object must you be in the sight of God who is of purer eyes than to behold iniquity; in whose sight the heavens are said to be unclean, and who charges his angels with folly! Now what can you do? How helpless! What do you desire? How guilty! What can you enjoy? How utterly unfit for heaven! You cannot dwell with God. You cannot commune with angels. You must, in your sins, be cast down to hell.

But the repentance of the sinner here may not be that of despair. Hope cheers the darkness, and chases away despair, when it is added, "Believe in the Lord Jesus Christ." If you abhor sin, and yourself on account of sin, then "look to the Lamb of God that taketh away the sin of the world." "He that believeth shall be saved."

This is God's work. And while it is committed, in the ministrations of the truth, to human agencies, our limits of knowledge and ability are placed where the power and excellency will be made to appear of God and not of man.

My dear child, I can point you to Christ, I can commend you to him, I can discharge my duty to you, and give you into his hands—there I must leave you. You must trust in him, you must believe in him. The act must be your own, and for yourself. I cannot believe for you. He cannot exercise that for you which can bring you peace, only as an act of your own distinctive and separate mind. You must exercise, by the aid of that divine agency which realizes to you your guilt—*you* must exercise faith in Christ.

Here I must leave you. To humble us, and show us that we are limited in power, and weak, we are left in obscurity, where the grace of God comes in to our relief, and where relief can come to him only who feels his weakness and dependence, and cries, in the exercise of faith in Jesus Christ, as a Saviour, "Lord, help me, or I perish."

Cherish, then, the influences of the Holy Spirit, feeling your dependence on divine teachings. Let not this favoured season of revival leave you in impenitence, hardened in sin. If you cannot see the whole process by which you are brought into a living and saving union to the Lord Jesus Christ, venture on his promises, and "feeling that you are a great sinner in the sight of God," plead, as you are authorized to do, his atoning blood, while you cast yourself on his grace.

## LETTER X.

### THE SINNER'S DIFFICULTIES AND DUTIES.

MY DEAR HARRIET,—Although the direction is plain and explicit, "Repent and believe in the Lord Jesus Christ, and thou shalt be saved,"—yet the sinner under conviction often finds himself surrounded with difficulties, which perplex his way, and retard his progress. He still asks, How shall I believe? His perceptions of truth are obscure, his definitions of them indistinct; and the finite being, who would lead the mind to rest, deeply feels that, which it is absolutely necessary should be felt by the inquirer himself, the necessity of divine teachings. God has been pleased to leave the work of regeneration so involved, that the excellency, the power, and the glory may be seen to be of God and not of man.

Many of the difficulties, however, which the sinner entertains in his own mind, and suffers to obstruct his way, are of his own imagining. Real difficulties are often overlooked, while the sinner is careless and unconcerned; but when awakened, nothing is more common than misguided fears, and ill-judged efforts, and unworthy apprehensions, and those views of duty which paralyze effort, and impede his progress in the truth.

When the sinner admits his dependence on divine influences, and feels his own weakness, he is disposed to apply this great and necessary truth to a fatal use, and conclude he has nothing to do. He therefore waits for impulses, and looks for the exercise of a divine agency, as the only moving power. He surrenders the glorious attributes of his moral constitution, and submits to be acted on, as if his mind, like his body, were material, and ruled by the same laws. But there are no divine agencies employed in the work of the sinner's conversion, which set aside his own agency. The Holy Spirit does not invade the freedom of the will, nor act but in accordance with the laws of the human mind. There are acts which belong appropriately and distinctly to the sinner which must be his own, and which no power can perform by substitution. He must repent and believe. These are voluntary acts of his own, and no invasion of his personal action will ever take place to produce them, independent of his voluntary agency.

Has God made it our duty to repent and believe in Christ? He has. Has he given us evidence of his sincerity in calling us to this duty? He has. He has laid in the plan a sure foundation for our salvation, and has realized its efficacy to all who have ventured on it. He has never said to any, "Seek ye me in vain." And yet he has said that he will be "sought unto"—and "they that seek shall find."

Do you then feel that you are a sinner, and as such justly exposed to the curse of the law? Act under this feeling. Has God called you to repentance? Repent. Has the word of unerring truth said, "Believe in the Lord Jesus Christ and thou shalt be saved?" Then "believe and be saved."

Here are plain practical duties attended with a blessing. They are plain—they are practical—prescribed by God—prescribed to us. No one who neglects these can find a blessing. Has ever any one who has obeyed, failed of the blessing? Not one. Duty then is plain. It is not for us to speculate, and object, and find fault. We are guilty. We are dying. God has told us what to do.

Go, my child, directly to God with your feelings. You can come to *me* with them. Go to your *heavenly* parent. You can confide in *me*. You can confide still more in *him*. You have acted under the impulse of feeling that has led you astray. Do not refuse to act under a safer feeling.

Perhaps you may be disposed to say that your

feeling is too weak or inconstant—that if you had more which would bear you through, or if it were unchangeable and permanent, you would commit yourself, and act under the direction of it. But do you never act on less important matters, and with less conviction of your own correctness, where you have no more feeling than now—and has not that feeling strengthened by exercise? And is this not the nature of all feeling? And will you refuse only in the best things to cherish your feelings, unless they are of power to control you? You have understanding also. Use that. Are you afraid of the consequences of sin? Oppose it.

There is no definable measure of feeling or conviction necessary to prepare you to carry your case to God. It is simply sufficient that you feel yourself to be a sinner, and that you are encouraged to come to Christ. Come then with the feeling and conviction that you have. Confess your sin to God. Have you difficulties? Tell them at a throne of grace. Dwell upon your sins. Set them in order before you. Hide them not from your own view. Have others expressed stronger feelings than you have? Do not, therefore, reject the least. It is enough if God, in infinite mercy, deigns to lead you, although in a way beset by difficulties. Does God call you? Say, "Here am I,"—and go, my child.

The blessings of God are often slighted because he does not bestow beyond measure. Others have felt and enjoyed more. But it is not those who have felt and enjoyed most, who hold on best to the end. Their very mercies puff them up, and prepare them for a fall; while those who are in more humble circumstances, by diligence and humility advance permanently and are safe. By diligence and perseverance, the snail may outstrip the rapid but inconstant deer.

Are you an awakened sinner? Bless God that you are not a careless sinner, that you are not in hell. Oh, think not lightly of a single feeling of awakening and conviction. Trifle not with the least indication of the Spirit's influence, as if you could recall it when it is gone. With an easy motion of the hand you might brush away from you a hair, a thread, a chain, let down from heaven, fastened to the throne of God; but when once so carelessly done, no power short of that which wheels and holds the planets in their orbits, could bring it again within your reach, could present it to your grasp. Lay hold on it while you can, and let not go.

## LETTER XI.

### THE SINNER'S DANGER AND DUTY.

My dear Harriet,—It is of great importance that we regard and treat God as sincere in his provisions and offers of mercy, that we act with simple sincerity in the use of the knowledge we have. Go to Jesus as a lost sinner, as soon as you feel that you are lost. Go to him as a willing Saviour, as soon as he offers himself as such. You feel that you are a sinner; that the law of God is good, even in its strictness, even in your condemnation. You feel it is necessary that law should operate through the universe of God, and under its operation your condemnation is necessary and just. You, then, are lost; you are helpless. In this condition you feel that Christ is such a Saviour as you need, able and willing. Do you feel all this, and are you willing to be saved by him? Then you meet him when you have these views and this feeling. You close with the terms of salvation here. No particular strength of feeling is necessary, if this be the real action of your heart. No amount of knowledge is necessary, except that you are a sinner, and Christ is an adequate Saviour. No ecstasies of joy are necessary; they will come in their proper time, but you need not be greatly concerned about them. Place the matter right between yourself and God. Many a redeemed sinner, I believe, has gone to heaven from a state of anxiety and doubt here, and has opened his eyes with surprise in glory. Others, I doubt not, have gone to a world of despair, from a state of false joy and false hope entertained here, surprised to find themselves the enemies of God.

You feel that you are a sinner, and would repent and believe if you could. Then do this. With the simplicity of a child go to a throne of grace, open all your heart to the Saviour, tell him all and speak freely. He hears. Tell him you are a sinner, and he is such a Saviour as you need —that you are in a lost and dying state—that you come to him for that deliverance which you can find no where else—that you give yourself helpless into his arms. Here make a formal surrender of yourself to Christ in soul and body, in all that you have and are, for time and for eternity, without any reserve. He who gave himself a ransom for sinners, who has convicted you by his Spirit, and taught you your need of him, is present to hear and to fulfil all he has engaged. If sincerely done on your part, if done heartily, and with no reservation, the record is on high, and will be read to your acceptance in the judgment day.

One caution let me urge upon you. Think not that a state of conviction has any merit in it. Beware of the impression that you are doing pretty well, because you are concerned for your soul. This very state of conviction, if it does not terminate in conversion, will add to your guilt. It only leads you to see more distinctly the duty for the neglect of which you will be condemned.

Think not that it is necessary you should suffer conviction of sin for any particular length of time. It is always your duty to repent and believe in Christ. The moment you are convicted of your sin by the Spirit of God, you see the force of obligation by which this duty is urged upon you. There is no necessity that its fulfilment should be delayed one moment. If you were thrown overboard, and were sinking in the angry waves, you would not feel that any length of time were necessary to convince you of your real danger, or to prepare you to lay hold on the rope thrown out to you. On the contrary, your danger would increase with the lapse of every moment, your strength would diminish, and your prospect of relief would lessen with every succeeding wave which beat over you. This is the real condition of the sinner. His case is every moment growing worse, while he continues in sin. Repent, then, now, and believe in Jesus Christ.

Beware, however, of a presumptuous hope, seized without an intelligent knowledge of the way of salvation. The plan is a simple one, as I have already defined it, and as you have often heard it described. When that is distinctly understood, proceed directly, and do not wait in expectation of an overpowering force of feeling to bear you away from the deliberate exercise of your reason. You feel that you are a sinner. You know that you are a sinner. Then say, in the impressive words of the sacred poem:

I'll go to Jesus, though my sin
  Hath like a mountain rose;
I know his courts, I'll enter in,
  Whatever may oppose.
Prostrate I'll lie before his throne,
  And there my guilt confess,
I'll tell him I'm a wretch undone,
  Without his sovereign grace.
Perhaps He will admit my plea,
  Perhaps will hear my prayer;
But if I perish I will pray,
  And perish only there.
I can but perish if I go,
  I am resolved to try,
For, if I stay away, I know,
  I must for ever die.

Do not permit yourself to go to Christ with a

demand. Think not that because there is no necessity that you should suffer conviction any length of time, you may of course find satisfaction at once. You have been a great sinner. You have resisted the invitations of God's word and Spirit. You may not be able to come at once with every suitable preparation of heart to receive the divine blessing. If you fail of it, the fault is yours. It lies not in the promise or provision of grace, but in your own heart.

What, then, is the part of duty and of propriety in a sinner, seeking the mercy of God? Plainly, to wait on God until he sends deliverance. "If you stay away you know you must for ever die." "You can but perish if you go." Resolve then, that if you must perish, you will perish at the foot of the cross. Did ever a poor sinner perish there? Never. It was there your dear father found mercy—not in ecstasies, but in the full and deliberate adoption of this very resolution.

Here, at the feet of Jesus, employ every means of knowing and doing your duty. Neglect no efforts, in the presumptuous expectation that miracles will be wrought to furnish you. Read, study, pray over your Bible. Avoid everything in company, conversation, or amusements, calculated to divert your mind from religion. Spend much time in private prayer and serious meditation, and let nothing separate you from your Saviour, until you have an evidence in the feelings and temper of your mind that you have cordially closed with the terms of mercy. Then you will be able to associate with the various objects which lie in the sphere of your duties in life, having the love and peace of God in your heart, and "whether you eat or drink, or whatsoever you do, you will be able to do all in the name of the Lord Jesus." Thus associated and exercised, with the conviction impressed on your experience, that "it is God that justifieth," you will go on your way rejoicing, and with the great apostle, will feel "persuaded that neither death, nor life, nor angels, nor principalities, nor powers, nor things present, nor things to come, nor height, nor depth, nor any other creature, shall be able to separate us from the love of God, which is in Christ Jesus our Lord."

## LETTER XII.

### EVIDENCES OF PERSONAL RELIGION.

My dear Mary,—When, in the anxiety and fears of a parent's full heart, I commenced, with prayer for a divine blessing, this series of letters, I hardly ventured to anticipate that I should so soon be permitted to address you as a child of God. So unexpectedly, I may say, have my expectations been fulfilled. The first hour of your birth, now fresh and present in my vivid recollection, was attended with a parental dedication of our child to God, which has ever been associated, in my mind, with something more than a general hope that the grace of God would, by covenant, reach this object of a father's and a mother's prayers. There is something attending on obedience to the expressed will of God, which brings us naturally into the attitude of expectants, and is attended, sometimes, I doubt not, by a divine impression of coming realities. Amid my fears, I seem to expect the conversion of my children to God; while, in the very exercise of this faith, I fear, with trembling, lest they may suffer the precious season of youth and of life to pass unimproved, or acting amid so many dangers, be deceived in their hope. I rejoice, my child, and give thanks to God for the hope which you express. But if you have truly given your heart to God, you have only performed the first act in a series of duties equally arduous and imperative, which reach on to the latest hour of your life, and take hold on your entrance to glory. These are to be considered and performed in detail as the only means of securing present peace, and an enduring "hope as an anchor to the soul."

The first thing, then, to be seriously considered by you, is the importance of doing thoroughly the great work of repentance. Religion is the great business of life, the one thing needful. All things else may be neglected without fatal loss, but "what can a man give in exchange for his soul?" The amazing difference of character among professing christians, as well as the fatal mistakes made by some, who utterly fail to maintain their hope, have their foundation laid in the very outset of their efforts in religion. I tremble when I see how hastily some young persons are encouraged by their religious teachers to entertain a hope, and how carelessly and inconsiderately many venture on a hope of mercy. Here is the place where fatal mistakes are made; not that mercy flows in a stinted stream, but that the fountain is mistaken, and the waters of death are deceptively substituted. Beware, be careful, be sure, my child, that you apply to the blood of Jesus, and abide under the droppings of the cross. "None but Jesus can do the dying sinner good."

One of your present evidences, then, that you have exercised saving repentance, is, that you are conscious you have found relief under conviction of sin in a view and acceptance of Jesus Christ, as your Saviour. Your own doings always deepen your conviction of guilt on every glimpse you take of them. You find hope and peace only as you contemplate Jesus Christ "wounded for your transgressions, bruised for your iniquities," and yourself as "healed by his stripes." You then lean entirely on him in your hope of pardon and acceptance. This is an important point in christian experience, and I would direct your attention to it with great urgency and solicitude. It is indeed the turning point in the experience of the true christian. The soul that flies to Jesus is safe —all others are lost. No matter how much conviction they may have had, or how great a load of guilt may have oppressed them, or how terrible their fears, or how confident their hopes that succeeded, if they have not been led to believe in, and receive, and rest entirely on Christ, as their substitute, to meet the penalty of the law, and to commit their salvation entirely to him, as their

Advocate on high, their hopes are all illusory. Their experience does not meet and coincide with the plan of salvation. It is only at the cross of Christ that the sinner can now have any adequate sense of the guilt of sin, and that only through the enlightening and convincing influences of the Holy Spirit, the divine Agent, who accompanies the cross. Christ must be ever before the sinner's mind, and furnish the comparison and contrast by which he measures and judges his own character, or the guilt of his sin. You must find, then, in your views of Christ as a Saviour, and in your sense of dependence, and actual reliance on him, in your "peace in believing, and your joy in the Holy Ghost"—you must find here your first and principal evidence of a saving change of heart.

Related to this experience, but fatally divergent from it, is a high state of excited feeling, often entertained under the effect of urgent external causes, producing strong but indistinct notions, fears deeply wrought, imaginings floating under the exciting effect of nervous irritation, and succeeded by a change necessary, because nature is exhausted. In persons of this class, are found no deliberate and intelligent views of sin in its awful sinfulness, of personal guilt in the sight of God, of Jesus Christ, offered as a propitiation for sin, and adapted to the sinner's case, no reaching forth to him, and reliance upon him as a Saviour. They have suffered fear, the fear of hell; they have trembled under the thought of being the enemies of God, because it is a terrible calamity to themselves; they have been acted on by sympathy, perhaps, seeing others also alarmed; they have suffered under their apprehensions, and wept, and swooned, and exhausted themselves with watchings, and high wrought animal excitement. The necessary change and quiet, which exhaustion produces, has been taken for conversion; while perhaps these very persons can give no "reason for the hope that is in them," no proper definition of sin, no adequate account of the way in which sin is pardoned, and the sinner is accepted. All is indefinite, all is cloudy and obscure, all is extreme in their feelings and professions, and nothing is satisfactory. These are usually the most confident in their professions, and severe in the judgments they pass on others, dogmatical in the peculiarities they adopt, and commonly the most unstable in their religious duty.

Another class of exercises, on which a religious hope is sometimes taken up, equally dangerous and fatal, is in the opposite extreme, where all this feeling and excitement are exchanged for a cold and philosophic speculation, where religion is made a mere mental operation, having its beginning and end, its foundation, whole experience and consummation in the principles of intellectual philosophy. In their dread of enthusiasm, this class of persons will extinguish their feelings, and in their zeal to exclude fanaticism, they forbid the exercise of zeal in religion. Religious experience with them is an intellectual exercise. "It plays round the head, but comes not near the heart." It is circumscribed in its exercise to formalities, to the Sabbath, to set phrases of speech, to "pomp and circumstance," to particular circles, and is never permitted to be introduced to offend the "ears polite" of men or women in the profanity of their rage, or sensual indulgence of their worldly pleasures. Thus dressed in buckram and starched and ruffled, religion is excluded from a free and social connection with the ordinary intercourse of life, and set conspicuously on the shelf, like the gilded Bible, and other books of forms, to be gazed at, and to show, as a kind of sign and seal, that "this family is religious."

## LETTER XIII.

### EVIDENCES OF PERSONAL RELIGION.

MY DEAR MARY,—Another evidence that you are "born again," will be found in the permanent character of the change, as exemplified in all the views you take of life, in your deliberate choice of companions and pleasures, and in all your intercourse with others. This life has formerly filled the field of your vision—has it not? Its pleasures, honours, possessions, connections, have bounded your views, and filled your desires. Now, a wider survey has opened. Eternity stretches out before you. Its pleasures, honours, possessions, and connections, occupy your thoughts and desires; while this life, with all that pertains to it, has dwindled to a point, and ceases to exert a leading influence on the great duties of your eternal course.

Your religion, if it be of any reality, will be carried modestly but with firmness into every department and duty of life. You will not be insensible to the danger of making a merit even of your duties, nor to the charge of ostentation, often, perhaps, captiously made by a censorious world, or by formal and heartless professors of religion. But you will be more afraid of provoking God by a neglect of duty, than of incurring the censure of men by a rigid performance of it. When performed with a proper spirit, you never need be ashamed of the charge of ostentation in the discharge of duty, and especially, as is sometimes the case, where there is no possibility of escaping the charge but by omitting the duty itself.

Sophronia, a young lady of my acquaintance, once left the paternal roof at an early age, and soon after she had entertained a hope in Christ, to finish her education at a boarding school. On her arrival at the place of her new residence, you will readily conceive she found new and peculiar trials in the new companions and duties with which she became necessarily connected. It produced a momentary struggle of mingled and various emotion. With her religion, religious duties, and religious character on one hand, and the world, with its various and counteracting influences on the other, she was brought to a stand; but she did not allow herself to hesitate. On the first morning after her arrival, she, with great civility, but firm determination, proposed to her room-mates to allow her the undisturbed occupancy of the chamber on a certain hour in the morning. It was granted. The struggle was over. She was a praying young lady. Here she was strengthened, and prepared to exert a most happy influence, as well as to feel the blessing of communion with God. What an influence was exerted by the decision of that hour! At the early age of twenty-two, I saw this young lady breathe out her soul in a most happy and triumphant death, after a short life of great purity and devotion. The greatest blessing, my daughter, which can be yours, is to die young, in the possession and exercise of a holy, religious faith.

Now look at the contrast of this picture in the story of Florida, related to me as a fact by another. It concerns a young lady, whose mind was awakened during a religious revival at a boarding school. She became serious, deeply serious. She even, I believe, entertained a hope. Soon she returned to her home again. There was an assemblage of her former companions for gay amusement—for a ball. She was invited—declined, was urged, importuned. Conscience spoke, and she persisted in her refusal. At length her father, yes her own father, advised her to go, and to continue her intercourse with her former companions. She declined. He urged it—No, she could not go. He would have enforced his wishes by authority, but that would not do. He employed this expedient. He promised her the most costly dress that could be purchased to deck her person if she would consent. The expedient succeeded. The dress was procured—she appeared that night in all the superiority and pride which it gave to her person. But it was the winding sheet to all her religious feelings and hopes. They fled from that hour—they never returned. Agitated and oppressed, she soon sunk into disease. She was laid on her death bed. She called her father—" Father," said she, " bring my gay dress." It was brought. " Hang it there before me." It was so suspended. With her eyes steadily fixed on that trifle, she said—" Father, see there the price of my soul "—and she died.

My daughter, your religious feeling must be thorough, all pervading, permanent, decisive, or it will be unfitted to sustain you in the conflicts and temptations of life—it will leave you to barrenness and spiritual darkness in death. This subject, in which I trust your dear sister now feels a personal interest as well as yourself, will be resumed in my next.

## LETTER XIV.

### STANDARD OF CHRISTIAN CHARACTER.

My dear Mary,—To be a christian, an heir of heaven, saved from hell—this is a distinction infinitely surpassing all others. It is a distinction which God alone can bestow, and which has been purchased for sinners at an infinite price. Do we talk of personal distinction then? Here is the highest which a sinner can possess. Do we desire personal favours? Here is the greatest which man can receive. Do we aspire to honours? Here is the only true and unfading honour. Would we be holy? Here is holiness. Would we be happy? Here is happiness—for "godliness with contentment is great gain"—and eye hath not seen, nor ear heard, nor hath it entered the heart of man to conceive, the blessedness that is in reserve for those who love God.

You hope, my child, that you are a christian! Then "all things are yours; whether Paul, or Apollos, or Cephas, or the world, or life, or death, or things present, or things to come;

all are yours, and you are Christ's, and Christ is God's." You hope that you are a christian. Then, you are not your own, "you are bought with a price." You hope you are a christian. Then this world is not your home—your "house is not made with hands; it is eternal in the heavens." You hope you are a christian. Then those who do the will of your Father in heaven, they are your mother, and sister, and brother. Be a decided christian. Be a whole christian. Be a christian, "not in word only, but in deed and in truth." You are not poor—you are rich, rich in Christ and his love, while you abide in him. You are honoured in his favour, holy in his righteousness to present you faultless before the throne of the Father, and by his grace to preserve you from temptation here; you are happy in the communion of his Spirit, and in the hope of glory. Be a christian indeed—devoted to Him who has "purchased you with his own blood;" having "your conversation and your heart in heaven," where your home and your treasure are; cherishing towards other christians the nearest relation, and the deepest love. I shall never lose a daughter, nor a daughter's love, because she loves me, first as a christian, and then as a parent. You will not be lost to the world when you live above it. You will not be lost to yourself, when you feel that you are "not your own."

You will lose nothing, when you give up all for Christ. You will have "great gain." You secure "the life that now is, and that which is to come."

My daughter, I desire to see you wholly devoted to Christ in heart and in life. Your parents gave you back to God in solemn and formal dedication when they received you from his hand. At a subsequent period, this dedication was renewed, and sealed with baptismal water, "the sign of the righteousness of faith." Your parents have ever held you as a sacred deposit, committed to our care and education here. We never held you as our own. On more than one solemn occasion, God intimated to us that your life was in his hands, and he would resume it—and we have assented. One prevailing desire ever predominated, and swelled our bosoms—that you might be his in this life, and be taken to himself in his own time and manner. And now that you have dedicated yourself to him, I desire that you should be an entire christian, and "serve the Lord wholly." Although you are endeared to me by the absence of your sainted mother, and doubly endeared by your voluntary surrender of your heart to God, I wish to call you mine in no sense, and would exert an influence on you in no way, which would divide your affections or embarrass your religious duty. I think I would not withhold you from the society of your dear mother, now in heaven, nor from any service to which He who has called you may appoint on earth. My only desire and anxiety is that you may be a devoted christian.

## LETTER XV.

### AIM AT HIGH ATTAINMENTS IN RELIGION.

My dear Mary,—The standard of your christian character will be decided at an early period in your christian course. We do not often rise above the grade to which we first aspire. Hence, the importance that you should, in the outset, have your mind fully possessed with the ardent desire to become an eminent christian. Next to the danger of self-deception, this is a subject of leading importance. Next to the "new birth," in order, is the formation of christian character. Our usefulness, our religious influence, and personal happiness, depend, first on the reality of our personal piety, and then on the maturity and perfection of that principle implanted by grace in the heart. God makes us, in christian character, what we desire to be made. He withholds from us no good thing.

Connected, then, with the very commencement of your christian course, I advise to a formal dedication of yourself, in soul and in body, in mind and strength, in all you have and are for time and eternity, to God. I advise you to make this dedication formal, to aid you in making it real. When you have duly, and without delay, considered the matter and prepared your heart for it, write down a form expressive of what you feel and desire, and determine, in the strength of the Lord, to do and to be. Let this instrument be signed by yourself, and placed under a succinct and clear account, carefully and conscientiously written, of your christian experience. Let this be done in the freshness of your early feelings, that in all your subsequent life you may recur to it, and see how you felt, and what you promised, when you entered into covenant with God. These two important records, the first headed: "My christian experience," and the second: "My self-dedication," may well stand at the head of your journal, or diary, which I hope you will keep for the remainder of your life. For an outline of the plan for the first record, I refer you to the memoirs of Mrs. Harriet Newell, in which she gives an account of her experience. For a general plan or form of self-dedication, I refer you to Doddridge's Rise and Progress.

I will now attempt to enforce this advice, by a brief sketch of the advantages of the plan proposed, and the objection which is sometimes urged against it.

In every enterprise, and on every subject, it

is important that we refer often to the point from which we started, and recur to first principles. Otherwise we are constantly liable to lose sight of the end at which we aim, and wander from our way. Our christian experience and our self-dedication associate us at once with the soul-inspiring scenes and transactions, which attended our first love. We go back to the childhood of our christian life, and revive all the associations with which it has been connected. The field, the tree, the book, the church, the garden, the chamber, the closet—there they stand before us, distinctly associated with the solemn scenes and impressive facts they witnessed. So this little manuscript spreads out before us in after life, and perhaps in distant lands, the mementoes of sacred and solemn parts of our history, which might otherwise have been forgotten. It is the sworn witness of our convictions, our confession, our solemn covenant with God; and like a familiar friend, it refreshes and quickens our memory by recounting the events and transactions in which we have been a party. These vivid feelings we need to cherish. They reprove our wanderings, and call us back to duty.

The practice of writing down our feelings and experience, from day to day, will aid us also in the important work of self-examination. Whenever we are about to define and record our feelings, we are brought to a careful examination of them. A loose and general expression will not be satisfactory. We record the present state of our minds. There it is—we read it, and see what we are.

The only objection which I have known to be urged against this practice, is, that we are apt to record stronger feelings than we have, and thereby deceive ourselves. This was my own conviction on the repeated examination of my journal, commenced when I entered on the christian life, and prosecuted for many years; and this impression under a peculiar state of feeling led me to throw the whole into the fire. I have been ever since convinced that I was wrong in this opinion, and have regretted the act to which it urged me. If I sometimes expressed my feelings too strongly, I have no doubt they were as often made against my religious character as for it, therefore not calculated to cherish a spiritual pride. I suppose the journal of your dear mother shared a similar fate, for I have often heard her express similar sentiments. She kept a journal, I know, for most of her life, but I have been unable to find it among her papers. I, therefore, earnestly advise you to keep your journal, and if you think at any time that any part of the past record is incorrect, make that opinion a part of your record at the time, and let the variant feelings of different days, months, or years, stand together. I can assure you their re-perusal will be instructive and profitable.

What do you now think a christian ought to be? That, no doubt, you now think you will attempt to be. The early record of these convictions, while they are fresh and vivid in the mind, will enable you hereafter to look at your standard when you may need a monitor. You have given yourself away to Christ. If your life is spared, you will not be exempted from the temptations inseparable from life. You will be compelled, in a course of christian duty, to meet with severe conflicts. You may be tempted to take back a part of what you now pledge and give to Him, who "has given himself for you." Your solemn covenant, then reviewed and renewed, may serve to strengthen and save you from dangerous or fatal compliances. Let the dedication of yourself to God, therefore, be deliberate, entire, formal, and often renewed.

You cannot serve God and mammon. Set it down as a truth always to be felt, that you must be entirely devoted in all the affections of your heart to the service of God, or your professions are a solemn mockery. There is no slavish service more oppressive than that which renders a sacrifice to the forms of religion where the spirit of devotion is wanting. If you would be personally happy, you must not attempt to quiet your conscience by a solemn form of religion, which leaves the heart entirely out of the service;

> " For God abhors the sacrifice,
> Where not the heart is found."

Your own personal happiness and usefulness depend much on the entireness of the present sur render you make of yourself, and the undivided service you devote to the cause of your Redeemer. You cannot be happy in a constrained service, and it will be constrained unless the full consent of the heart gives direction to it. You cannot be useful where the principal energies of the soul are opposed to objects you professedly pursue. Religion itself, in its general character and influence, will suffer through your example. You will have lived in vain, and, dying unfurnished for the world to come, will be disappointed of that reward in another life which is promised only to those who " live godly in Christ Jesus."

On the other hand, how calm and full of consolation is a consistent christian! How dignified and full of salutary influence is his life! He is honoured by those who find no communion with him. There is something like sublimity in his course. He respects himself, and is respected by others. He honours God and is promoted to honour. Be careful, then, to deal honestly with yourself when you renounce the world as your portion, and venture on the christian's hope. Let sincerity and an entire devotedness pervade every action. In fine, be a christian,—this is all. If you are such, you will not fail to be every thing else that will be essential to your true interest. Without this character you must be miserable, possess what else you may.

## LETTER XVI.

### EMINENT PIETY.

My dear Mary,—To be a christian is the highest distinction and privilege that can be conferred on a mortal. But this term itself is rendered somewhat generic by its application to the various classes of christians of whom we are accustomed to speak. Some are satisfied with the distinctive appellation of a Christian, as expressive of a religious system, in opposition to a Mahommedan, a Brahmin, &c. Some are very tenacious of a sectarian name among the many denominations, who embrace the christian religion. But leaving these distinctions, I mean by a christian a true disciple of Christ the Saviour of sinners, the only distinction in religious character which will be of any final benefit to us. I wish you, my daughter, to be such a christian, a real christian. In this class I desire, also, that you may not be satisfied with being barely a christian, with just piety enough to save you; not a slothful, cold, inefficient, joyless christian, but an eminent christian.

If you are truly a christian, you will feel it is not only desirable that you should be saved, but that others also should be saved. You will not be satisfied without doing something to effect this desirable object; for what we greatly desire, we seek by our personal efforts to promote. To this end you will seek to be an eminent christian—not eminent by a great name, but eminent by the possession and exercise of great grace, by the production of great good to the world. It is not necessary to the true blessedness of this distinction that you should be extensively known, but only that you should have in your own soul a living principle of religion deeply implanted, and glowing—that you should be laborious, active, and efficient in imitation of our divine Redeemer, who went about doing good, that you may thereby contribute to promote the great end of his sufferings and death, viz: "to bring many sons unto glory."

You may pass through life without disgrace in a mere profession of religion; but do you tremble at the thought of the dangers to which you are exposed? Do you desire to be distinguished among the number of those who shine as lights in the world, and are useful to their fellow men? Do you seek for a near communion with the Saviour, for bright proof of your adoption, for the anchor hope in trials and storms, for the quiet approbation of a good conscience and approving brethren in Christ, or for a martyr's crown if persecutions must make a trial of your faith? Then you must be an eminent christian. Not for one possible event of life, but for every event you will need the aid, support, or protection of eminent piety.

For that character which is so necessary to your safety and happiness, the gospel provides. Yes, the gospel requires eminent piety, even perfection. Perfection is the consummation of the christian character, which is accomplished when he is admitted to that state for which this character fits him. Here, however, the christian character is progressive, and in this change from one degree of grace to another, we find the excitement so well fitted and necessary to our present state. The standard of christian character, constantly presented as the object of our effort, is perfection, and He that hath begun a good work in us will carry it on to perfection. Wherever, then, we may place the absolute completion of the work of grace, eminent piety is an attainment which belongs to time, and may be predicated of any period in the christian's life. The attainment of it does not require that we should be absolutely sinless, which we, by our own consciousness, know we are not.

That which is required by the Bible, is also rendered necessary by the circumstances in which we are placed. We are surrounded by temptations—Oh, how numerous, insidious, and strong! The aged saint, as he stands on the verge of eternity, and sees the young and inexperienced come forward to enter on the christian life, amid his joys betrays emotions of apprehension and anxiety. Why? He reflects on the dangers which throng the path he has trod, and which is to be travelled by the inexperienced feet of these now weak and perhaps too self-confident disciples. He reflects that many of those who commenced with him, have made shipwreck of their faith, have been left far behind, have faltered and perhaps tired, and "have walked the ways of God no more." He recurs to his own discouragements and misgivings, and wonders that he has persevered, wonders that any persevere to the end. I well recollect that at a critical period of my christian life, full of hope, expectation, and joy, I saw nothing before me but brightness and glory, such an aged saint, deeply interested in my welfare, appeared thus pensive and sad, when the peculiar ceremonies of the time called, as I thought, for cheerfulness and congratulation. In the varied experience of my subsequent life, I have frequently recurred to that hour, and had vividly presented to my mind that pensive and expressive countenance, which seemed to say, when

I saw no change, "Take care, young man, your history is not yet written—who knows whether you will die a wise man or a fool?" I shall never forget that look. I cannot lose sight of that countenance. It seemed to doubt me. It beamed upon me like the third question applied to Peter by his Master, "Lovest thou me?" It grieved me. My daughter, you are beginning life amid temptations. I know not—you know not, to what you may be exposed. Oh, the yearning of a father's heart asks for you this protection of character, that you may be eminently pious!

To regulate the mind and direct its energies to profitable effort, you will need a vigorous pulsation and healthful moral action in the heart. Eminent piety alone will answer the great demands of your circumstances in life. This alone will prepare you for the service to which you are called. To live in this age of the church, too, and in a protestant country, is a privilege, but a privilege which demands of you a service that can be discharged by no powers you have or can bring to your aid, without eminent personal piety. The age in which we live demands of individual christians peculiar labours and efforts, for which high religious character is required. The missionary cause is to be sustained by personal labours and sacrifices; and the various benevolent operations to which the church is pledged need eminent qualifications in christians to sustain them. Without this eminent piety to meet a peculiar demand, the light which has already streaked the horizon, and been hailed as the millennial dawn, will retreat, and leave the world again to moral darkness and disappointment.

But without regard to the great objects of public benevolence, in which the church is engaged, and on which every individual christian exerts a share of influence, nothing but eminent piety will prepare you for the faithful, efficient, and profitable discharge of domestic duties which will devolve upon you. You are a daughter, a sister, a pupil—in all these relations, and as a member of the school and family, you have responsibilities and duties, which nothing can prepare you to meet in the best manner but a spirit of piety that shall be all-pervading. Your own personal happiness, and the happiness of those with whom you daily associate, will be intimately involved in the spirit you habitually cherish, and the manner in which these duties are performed. I shall, at another time, remark on these several classes of domestic duties; at present I only allude to them to say, what an awakened attention to the history of families and persons within your knowledge will at once impress on your conviction, that nothing but eminent piety can prepare you for the duties and responsibilities of your domestic relations. I need not tell you how intimately the happiness of your surviving parent rests on his children; how much you can do to help or interrupt the peace and harmony of our little family, by your intercourse with your sister and brother; how sensibly you may affect the comfort of your teachers; how important is the example of one young lady at school on all her schoolmates; or how powerful is the reflex influence on her own peace, happiness, and character, constantly exerted by all she does. Nothing but ardent piety can prepare you to meet the present duties which devolve upon you, leaving out of the account those which will be added as you advance in years, and the circle of your relations enlarges.

To be useful in the world, you must aim at and make high attainments in piety. Few, except those of this character, have proved to be a blessing to the church. Many of those who profess religion, are a mere incumbrance to that sacred cause, which every one should seek to recommend to others, by a holy walk. The humblest christian may exert a strong influence. Piety is efficient. You may exert this influence. Every christian may do this. It is his duty, and exerted, it is efficient on all who take knowledge of him. None live alone. "No one," therefore, as the apostle says, "liveth to himself." We may exert our influence on one. If that one is saved by our instrumentality, we do vastly more than the great, the rich, or the learned man, who hides his light, or dishonours his profession; for he thereby prejudices that cause he is bound to defend and help.

We cannot enter heaven without eminent piety. Our souls must be absorbed in the subject of religion. Jesus must be the enrapturing object of our vision, and of our thoughts—the love of God must fill our hearts, and a growing benevolence towards all men must control the energies of our whole nature, or we cannot enter heaven. Are we willing to live with a bare hope, to save us from despair, and put off all this glorious work of sanctification, which is the appropriate work of time, to the very last moment of life when we are to be glorified? Oh let "the love of Christ constrain us, because we thus judge, that if Christ died for all, then were all dead: and that he died for all, that those who live should not henceforth live unto themselves, but unto him who died for them and rose again." "Grow in grace and in the knowledge of our Lord and Saviour Jesus Christ." "If ye be risen with Christ, seek those things which are above, where Christ sitteth at the right hand of God."

## LETTER XVII.

### THE INFLUENCE OF SETTLED PRINCIPLES.

My dear Children,—Notwithstanding the confidence I feel in your judgment, filial affection, good resolutions, and even stronger defences to a virtuous, if not a religious life, the solicitude of a parent's heart is awakened by what he knows of the dangers and temptations of life, yet to be encountered by your inexperienced feet. I cannot be always with you. Exigencies will inevitably occur in life, where you must be called to independent, personal decisions, perhaps pressed suddenly upon you, and calling for immediate action in the presence of temptation, plausible and inviting, but fatal to the taste and to the touch. Ah, these are the turning points in life, which often give the most important direction to the whole future course. Many have gone successfully through, simply because they have never encountered them. Others have been led in the right way, because judicious and pious friends have borne them along. None have been always wise by intuition, or by inherent power.

Could I give you a moral map of life, and define to you the points where danger lies concealed, where your decision, and resolution, and special efforts will be called in requisition, you might be more safe. But the greatest dangers are the most insidious. The tempter is always plausible. "It is not to vice, surrounded with her appropriate symbols of cruelty, impurity, and misery; associated with the grossest absurdities, dissevered from all the plausibilities and proprieties with which refinement and gayety have crowned her head and shrouded her deformities, that we are in danger of doing homage. But it is to vice, when 'clad in decencies;' to vice 'when elegantly dressed and well perfumed;' to vice, when she occupies the border country between right and wrong; to vice, when she presents herself with all the form and lineaments of virtue, but bears about with her all the heart, and spirit, and life-giving principle of corruption, that we are tempted to bow the knee, and pay the tribute due only to her whose complexion she borrows, and whose throne she usurps."

"The grace of God," by which true christians are "kept through faith unto salvation," is not exerted against the consent of the will, nor independent of the moral agency of the sinner constantly employed in the use of means, by which that grace is procured. This life is a "warfare"

—we are co-workers with God—and are exhorted to "give all diligence to make our calling and election sure." We are to be assiduously engaged, then, in self-discipline, education, and defence. The work is ours, and our attainments and triumphs are proportioned to our diligence, activity, and perseverance. Your attention will be necessary, first to principles, and then to habits formed on the application of those principles. You cannot be pious and good in the gross or aggregate, without attention to duties in detail. Your principles must be applied. In this way you become familiar with them, and they are proved when thus drawn out into practice. I will endeavour to show you what I mean. Your principle will not allow you to violate the truth. I will suppose you have repeatedly looked at this in the abstract, but no distinct opportunity has occurred for the practical application of it. At length such an occasion arrives. You are tempted to falsehood. Advantages are offered—flattering rewards are held out to you. Perhaps a falsehood may hide a fault, prevent a merited rebuke, may gain a friend. Can you tell a lie? No, you cannot. You are principled against it. There is no hesitation—no balancing of arguments. You say at once—"I cannot do this thing, and sin against God." The same may be said in regard to taking what is not your own, profaneness, Sabbath-breaking, or any other sin enumerated in the decalogue. You have settled it deeply in principle, in deliberate view of all the consequences of sin, in the self-reproach which attends it, the shame to which it exposes, and the wrath of God that certainly follows, that you cannot "consent to sin." When the temptation occurs, the principle is applied, and character is proved.

You see, then, what principle is. It is an affection of the soul, settled, of uniform action, and unyielding integrity. It often triumphs over vice, presented to beguile us with all its blandishments, and force of appeal to the passions, and present gratification. We know, therefore, how it will operate, and to what results it will lead. When these principles have been applied so as to have formed a character, it is pronounced with certainty that that person will act in a certain way on a given subject, because his principles are known. It is known he will tell the truth, and therefore we rely on what he says. We know he will scrupulously respect the rights of property, and therefore we trust him. We know he will regard the holy Sabbath, will honour his parents, &c. As he is trusted and confided in for his integrity, he will be saved from many temptations: for wicked men will not dare to approach him with their solicitations. Once severely rebuked, vice retires, or repeats its solicitations with greater hesitancy; while it approaches with a bolder front and greater confidence, where it has once been listened to, or entertained.

The importance, then, of defining and settling our principles of action may be easily seen. It both gives us a confidence in ourselves, and gains to us the confidence of others. This is no less true in morals than in science, or any other department of practical life. I will illustrate by an example. In a recent examination which I attended at your school, a young lady was called upon to solve a difficult question in Algebra. She went to the black board with a modest confidence, stated the question, and the principles on which the demonstration was founded, and after an abstruse process, she came out with the wrong answer. She, without embarrassment, blotted out the whole, and proceeded on the same principles with a similar process, but with the same result. She then reviewed the work as it stood, and not detecting the error, became a little confused—not because she doubted her principles, or herself, but perhaps at the thought of the public exhibition of herself to strangers. Her teacher then said, "I have confidence in Miss K., that she will accomplish the work. Her premises are correct, and I have never known her fail to accomplish whatever she has undertaken in the application of them." The young lady again rallied her confidence, and by a glance of the eye discovered in the work that she had, perhaps, placed *plus* instead of *minus*, which she hastily corrected and arrived at the true answer.

Our principles being right, and persevered in, will sustain us in the result; well settled and defined, they will inspire us with confidence, and excite us to perseverance. Correct principles, faithfully practised, will lead to a successful issue. They may embroil us in difficulties, and the demonstration may come through an abstruse process; but it will come. Sometimes a falsehood may save us from great difficulties, in which the truth will involve us; but it will never bring out the right answer. In the final proof we shall be put to confusion. So in every thing—in morals —"the light of the wicked shall be put out, and the spark of his fire shall not shine,"—but "the righteousness of the upright shall deliver him."

## LETTER XVIII.

### PRINCIPLES APPLIED.

My dear Children,—No difficulties in which our principles may involve us, should ever induce the least relinquishment of them. Principles can never be compromised—this makes a man of integrity. But some, by their practice, say opinion must never be modified by circumstances, nor submit to facts—this makes an obstinate man. The former is the terror of his enemies, the latter a burden to his friends. Difficulties sometimes are inseparable from the duty itself—sometimes it is the result of our own mistakes, and easily corrected by a careful review. In either case the only remedy is a strict adherence to the principle in a persevering application of it to the end. It is wise sometimes to yield a point, but always fatal to abandon a principle. To distinguish the cases accurately in the varied intercourse of life, often constitutes the difference between the man of popular and the man of repulsive manners, and gains to the one an access and influence among men, from which the other, with the best and purest motives of action, perhaps, is effectually debarred. We should always seek to present the most important principles to the acceptance of others, recommended by the least repulsive and most attractive forms. It is not necessary, for instance, that my neighbour should stand, or sit, or kneel in prayer, but it is absolutely necessary he should pray; and I will yield to his prejudices, his ignorance, or his caprice, in sitting, or standing, or kneeling, if he will consent to pray. So, if I can persuade him to receive and obey the gospel, I will not contend with him about forms and ceremonies—he may be an Episcopalian, Presbyterian, Baptist, or Methodist.

The manner in which principle should be sustained is illustrated in an anecdote of Latimer, a distinguished minister of the gospel, in the reign of the Eighth Henry of England. When called to preach before the tyrant, his royal master, he assailed, and pointedly reproved those sins by which that monarch was disgraced. Stung by the reproof, the sovereign appointed him to preach on the next Sabbath, in the royal presence, and required him to retract publicly what he had said. Latimer, accordingly, ascended the pulpit, amid the gaze of the royal retinue, and surrounded by the splendors of the greatest court in Europe. The good man is said to have commenced with this soliloquy;—"Now, Hugh Latimer, bethink thee, thou art in the presence of thy earthly monarch; thy life is in his hands, and if thou dost not suit thyself to his fancies, he will bring down thy gray hairs with blood to the grave. But Hugh Latimer, bethink thee, thou art in the presence of the King of kings and Lord of lords, who hath told thee, 'Fear not them that kill the body, and after that have no more that they can do; but fear him who, after he hath killed, hath power to cast into hell!' Yea, I say, Hugh Latimer, fear Him." He then repeated all he had said on the preceding Sabbath, and enforced it with additional and personal appeals. The angry monarch sent for the faithful minister, and exclaimed, "How durst thou insult thy monarch so?" Latimer replied, "I thought if I were unfaithful to my God, it would be impossible to be loyal to my king." The king, self-convicted, embraced the man of principle, and replied, "Is there yet one man left who is bold and honest enough to tell me the truth?"

The manner in which adherence to principle will sustain a man, may be illustrated in the history of Luther, the Reformer. Cited by the ecclesiastical tyrant who then filled the Papal throne, to appear and answer for his alleged heresies, he boldly replied to his friends, who feared for his safety, "I am called by the providence of God, and I will go and answer for his truth, though I should be opposed by as many devils in the way as there are tiles on the buildings." With such a spirit he conducted, and was a principal instrument in effecting the Reformation.

The subject may find a still more impressive illustration in the example of the three children, who refused to bend the knee, and pay their homage to the image, which Nebuchadnezzar, the king, had set up. They were, by order of the king, cast into the burning fiery furnace; but one, like unto the Son of God, was seen to walk with them in the midst of the fire, and he led them forth, and not a hair of their head was burnt. And this is in accordance with the promise of God to his people, "When thou passest through the waters I will be with thee; and through the rivers, they shall not overflow thee: When thou walkest through the fire, thou shalt not be burnt, neither shall the flame kindle upon thee."

## LETTER XIX.

### FORMATION OF HABITS.

My dear Children,—Your self-control, as well as entire character, will depend on the early formation of right habits. Principle lies at the foundation of all character. The fundamental and pervading principle of religion, is love to God. It secures a respect for, and obedience to, all his commands; and carried out in the practical duties of life, it forms our habits.

Influenced by love to God, I will suppose as an example, we adopt the rule expressed in the ninth commandment. With this principle and rule of life, we enter on our trial. We are called to testify, and, in the application of our rule, we tell the truth—but this act is not a habit. We are then called repeatedly to speak, and, under temptations of various kinds and degrees, to swerve from the truth—we adhere to our principle. Here a habit is formed. A habit is the succession of like actions, or a uniform action on any one subject. Habit, then, is the action of principle, and is the development of it to the observation of others. It also strengthens and defends our principles, as it gives us confidence in ourselves, and a triumph over temptations. Hence the importance of forming right habits.

There is one respect in which the formation of right habits is important, in proportion as they do *not* involve important principles. Our characters, and usefulness, and happiness, are often deeply affected and injured by some trifling habit, which has been permitted to become immovably fixed, because it was originally supposed to violate no moral obligation. A gentleman may chew tobacco, or a lady may take snuff, until the habit may become deeply, injurious to character, usefulness, and happiness, and withal unconquerable. A young lady may become careless in her wardrobe, or fantastical and vain in her dress, until her character, usefulness, and happiness, all become involved and ruined in one bad habit. A little girl may be petulant, complaining, and unaccommodating towards her sister or brother, until mutual alienation and distrust prove to her, too late, how ruinous one bad habit may prove to be, when persevered in. And yet, perhaps, the persons whose character, usefulness, and happiness have been thus self-destroyed, could not be tempted to the commission of a bold sin nakedly exposed.

My present object, however, is not so much to pursue this train of remark, as to give a direction to your habits on some of the most important religious duties, on which I feel an ardent desire that you should, at the present time, adopt correct views, and pursue a decided course of habitual action.

The first habit which you should seek to form, is that of a punctual attention to daily religious duties. You have been early taught the prayers appropriate to a state of childhood, and have no doubt preserved a habit of repeating them. But your present years and greater maturity of understanding demand something more, to which I trust you are urged by your own convictions and sense of duty. In the right formation of this habit, and perseverance in it, the christian finds his vigorous growth and lively religious feeling to be deeply involved, while it will also aid the serious mind in his inquiries after truth in every stage of his anxious efforts.

The particular points of religious duty to which I wish now to direct your attention, as calling for a place in your daily exercises, are reading the scriptures, private meditation, self-examination, and prayer.

Reading the scriptures as a daily duty and privilege is necessary, if we would act with caution and wisdom in the most important and momentous concerns. Suppose you were travelling in the night through an unknown and dangerous road—you would seek a guide to direct you, or a light to discover the way. Or if you should call at a great inn to sojourn for a night, where every sort of lodgers were assembled, you would not undertake, even for once, to find your chamber, where you might pray and lie down to rest, without a lamp or guide to direct your inexperienced step, amid various stair-ways, and a multitude of apartments, occupied by strangers of every variety of character. Such a lamp to our feet, and such a guide to our paths, is the holy Bible. In this world, where we have no continuing city, through which we pass as pilgrims, and over which moral and mental darkness prevails, we can find no adequate light to direct us but in the scriptures. We cannot proceed on our journey for a single day with safety, destitute of our guide. Diverging paths on the right hand and on the left, all marked by fresh footsteps, or crowded with travellers, constantly distract our attention, and shake our confidence. We need a guide who is worthy of all trust, and to whom we may direct the question, "Which way shall we go?" All cannot be right, and yet each invites our company. We need a lamp, lest, when night comes on, we miss our path, and become irretrievably lost. That only light, that only guide, is the Bible.

Our only rule of faith and guide in practice, is

the Holy Spirit, speaking to us in the scriptures of the Old and New Testaments. You can confide in no other book—you must not trust the best man on earth. If an angel of light should profess to teach you contrary to the word of God, you must not listen—you must pronounce him a liar. Such an experiment was fatally tried on the mother of all our race. The tempter "said unto her, Thou shalt not surely die." And the fallen angel, who thus deceived our mother, is still employed in the same malignant purpose. He has agents seeking, under every imposing and deceitful form, to discredit the word of God. Repel him, I entreat you, in every form, whether he comes in the imposing character of God's priest, to take away from you your Bible and substitute his living instructions, the interpretation of the church; or in the vision of new revelations, superseding the written word. I say to you, my children, hold on to your Bible. Bring every teacher "to the law and to the testimony," if they speak not according to this word, it is because there is no light in them. "Believe not every spirit, but try the spirits whether they are of God, because many false prophets are gone out into the world."

The evidences which assure us that the Bible is the word of God are taught in your classes. To these you have already given some attention, and will give still more. The object of these instructions is to assure you that God has indeed spoken to us in his holy word of the Old and New Testaments. We must hear God speak—and that is the end of controversy. Here he speaks in the Bible, which is always the same. When you have once admitted the evidences of this, "here is the judge that ends the strife." Whoever speaks, then, open your Bible. A child may read that. A child may understand that. Try the man or angel that would teach you, by that Bible. Is he a priest? The fallen spirit, who can assume the appearance of an angel of light, may also make use of a wicked priest to deceive you. And what fitter instrument of deception could he find than a priest, the professed "legate of the skies?" And where would a wicked man, instigated by the devil, sooner go than into the priesthood, especially if that priesthood should be so organized as to gratify a worldly ambition? I would encourage you to cherish and respect a holy ministry, devoted to their holy work. God forbid that I should weaken, in the hearts of my daughters, a respect for this means of God's appointment to bring sinners to repentance, and to edify the church. But the worst men in the world have appeared as the professed ministers of our holy religion; and we are divinely taught, that he who is emphatically called "the man of sin," shall come under cover of this very profession—who "shall depart from the faith, giving heed to seducing spirits and doctrines of devils, speaking lies in hypocrisy; forbidding to marry, and commanding to abstain from meats, which God hath created to be received with thanksgiving of them which believe and know the truth"—"the son of perdition, who opposeth and exalteth himself above all that is called God, or that is worshipped; so that he as God sitteth in the temple of God, showing himself that he is God; whose coming is after the working of Satan with all power and signs and lying wonders; and with all deceivableness of unrighteousness in them that perish, because they received not the love of the truth that they might be saved."

I say, therefore, my children, go to your Bible for instruction. Permit no power on earth to take the precedence of your Bible to instruct you finally in duty. You are not to permit even your father to do it. I dare not do it. Let no man be the keeper of your consciences. As no man can answer for you to God, so no one can interpret the word of God to you against your own conscientious convictions, nor assume your responsibilities as intelligent moral agents. I cannot do it. And if I cannot, who can? I act for you in your infancy, instruct you in your childhood, and, having discharged my duty, now place you on your responsibility, under the light of God's revealed will. I say again, make the Bible your daily study. The manner in which this may be done to the greatest profit, will be made the sub ject of some further instructions.

## LETTER XX.

### DAILY READING THE BIBLE.

My dear Children,—The Bible, as our rule of faith and practice, is to be read and studied. It is to be studied that we may become persuaded of its authenticity and divine inspiration, that we may possess ourselves of its historical stores of learning, its divine doctrines and precepts, its moral sentiments and illustrations. It should be read daily, also, for the same purposes—but prin cipally to aid our devotions. The daily reading of the scriptures, attended with meditation, self-examination and prayer, is necessary to the preservation of a lively religious frame, and to the attainment of that knowledge which is good and "profitable to direct."

This habitual reference to the inspired writings is necessary to preserve in our minds a distinct view of divine things. Nothing else will do it. We are driven into the field of speculation; we travel amid shadowy forms of truth, under every other tuition. We see, at most, in the descriptions of good men, in the most glowing ministry of truth—we have only the bright pictures of those eternal realities, to which the mind reaches and aspires; but here, in the scriptures, we have the very image of the things. We sit down to behold, as in a mirror, the Sun of righteousness, reflecting light upon our path, the glories of redemption, as they are seen in the face of Jesus Christ. God speaks in his word. Sometimes a holy man or an angel may help us to understand it; but as a common rule, it is best without note or comment, where it is left to explain itself, and to quicken our powers by the effort to compare and educe the true meaning.

This constant application of the word of God to our daily experience, is also necessary to exert a modifying influence on all the objects of desire with which we are conversant. It tells us plainly what the world is, and often reverses the decisions we make on its possessions. It tells us what we are, and contradicts our opinions of ourselves. It shows us what time is, and contracts it from its unlimited or indefinite duration, and shows it to be but a point. It discriminates character, and regulates our choice of companions. It brings the possessions of this world into direct connection with its fleeting and limited duration, and lifts our affections from these fading forms, which before appeared like durable realities.

It administers reproof. There it is, unaltered,

unchangeable. It knows no accommodation to circumstances. It admits no compromise. Its principles are distinctly marked, defined and unyielding. We cannot read and apply them without reproof. A friend may, and almost necessarily will, be influenced by personal considerations and circumstances. His feelings are enlisted. His prejudices, fears, prepossessions, are all present to give colour to his peculiar manner of presenting the truth to us. But the word of God, when we consult that alone, knows no form of accommodation. If we are faithful to apply the caustic, it comes in its unmodified and unmixed power, in a direct operation upon our proud flesh, and must bring the diseased parts to a healthy action. It is profitable for instruction. The Saviour spake as never man spake. His teachings are here recorded. Holy men of old spake as they were moved by the Holy Ghost. Thus taught, they have here recorded the truth revealed to them. Therefore, it is said, "All scripture is given by inspiration of God, and is profitable for doctrine, for reproof, for correction, for instruction in righteousness."

It corrects all our other knowledge, and all mistakes in our estimation of other truths. A scholar, in the pursuit of human science, is extremely apt to take those truths he investigates, separate from God, and consider his learning in immediate and constant reference to himself and this world. The scriptures, constantly consulted, will lead him always to estimate all truth in reference to God, and in view of his own relation to God and eternity; and in all his investigations of nature, he will "look through nature up to nature's God." His own pride of intellect will constantly be checked in the comparisons here drawn, and a moral influence will be exerted on all his feelings by this reference of all truth to the great eternal and unalterable standard.

The influence of divine truth is necessary to instruct, reprove, and correct, every day, and under all circumstances; to bring us under the controlling power of eternal realities, and to modify all our views of present things. I hope you do not need to have motives multiplied, as they easily might be, to induce you to make the Bible the only standard of your faith, the man of your counsel, your manual, your daily companion. In making a few remarks on the manner in which the Bible should be read, I shall be directed chiefly by my own practice, adopted on experience.

First, I advise you to read all the Bible. I do not mean by this that you should task yourselves to read it once, and then confine your attention to particular portions for ever afterwards. Let your customary reading embrace the whole Bible, so, that in due time you will review the whole. It is a beautiful harmony which ought ever to be embraced and viewed together in all its parts. This forms one of the evidences of its divine original Every part of the Bible ought to be read by you, at least once a year.

But although all parts of the Bible are profitable, they are not all equally profitable at all times, nor profitable to the same ends. For devotional purposes, the historical and some other parts are less adapted. The Psalms of David breathe the most elevated spirit of devotion—and the Epistles unite the most glowing devotion with doctrinal views and propositions. The Evangelists and Acts of the Apostles will, of course, be made very familiar to every habitual reader of the Bible. But the Psalms and Epistles are best suited to devotional purposes, and may be generally, although they should not be exclusively, used.

Portions of scripture, which embrace a single subject, should be read at once, that the connection may be seen. It is well, if time permit, to read a whole epistle at one sitting. Read with references, and examine carefully parallel and corroborating texts, that the scriptures may be allowed to explain themselves. Commit favourite and the most impressive texts, and chapters, and whole books, to memory. This was a habit, long pursued, of your dear mother. She committed to memory, in this way, almost the whole New Testament. The treasure was more valuable to her than gold or silver. It gave her often an advantage, both in public and in private, most important and enviable. It was her design that a part of your education should embrace this same exercise of the memory. I hope your hearts are now so affectionately disposed toward divine truth that you will be impelled to imitate your beloved mother in this respect, and thus fulfil her and my own desire.

When you read your Bible, mark those passages which you wish to commit to memory, or which appear particularly impressive. You can then easily recur to them, and when your time is limited, you can readily direct your reading to portions the most expressive and profitable. As the study of the Bible will form a separate subject, I will now leave you to reflect on some of the motives here urged which should lead you to a daily reading of the scriptures, and the manner in which that reading may be most profitably conducted.

## LETTER XXI.

### PRIVATE MEDITATION.

My dear Children,—In the daily reading of the scriptures for the purposes of devotion, you will find private meditation absolutely necessary to any great proficiency, or intelligent and permanent peace. The Bible reveals divine truth. That truth believed and entertained in the mind is the foundation of joy, greater or less, in proportion to the clearness of our perception, and the confidence with which it is received as the word of God. Having received the Bible in all its parts, as given to us by divine inspiration, it is necessary that its communications should be well considered, should be made the subjects of our careful examination, and that our hearts should be formed in the spirit of its truths, by frequent and long meditation upon them.

Possibly there never was so much real piety in the church as now. But this has been justly characterized as a day of action. On all subjects, and especially on religion, there is a spirit of enterprise, leading forth the benevolent as well as the mercenary and ambitious to explore new fields of gain or beneficence, and directing all the energies of the mind to practical effect. The effect of this peculiar character of the age, is to call the student from his study to mingle in the current of public feeling and effort. In this fact, we may undoubtedly find the true cause, which has originated the taste for bold speculation in theology, and jostled us somewhat out of the precise forms of our old systems, elaborate creeds, and established technicalities. The labour-saving principle is applied to everything. Men are not satisfied now with travelling at the dull rate of a former century, or effecting results in physics by the slow process of ordinary means. When these novelties are applied to religion, and the ark of the Lord, for which the church seems to have been preparing a new temple, is committed to these bold spirits, good and thoughtful men tremble for its safety, and fear the results. But the church has a promise of more glorious days, and they are doubtless to come as the result of human instrumentalities. Improvements must come with changes. Try every new theory and new measure with great caution. Reject not a theory, or a measure, merely because it is new, nor be immovably wedded to any system, because it has the sanction of names or of age. The latter course makes bigots, the former, fanatics; the latter has made the Roman Catholic church what it is, the former has originated all the extravagances, which mere sectarian zeal and ignorant empiricism has introduced to distract and degrade the church.

The church, when she comes to the victories of the last times, forgetting party names, and party or sectarian forms, will go forth in any measures, and with any instrumentality, by which "the truth" can be made to tell on the conscience and reach the heart. Such a union and effort in the church, I hope my children may see, although I may not; and the suggestions here made are suited to the consideration of all, even the youngest in the church; when, as in this day, all must necessarily be theologians.

In this call to action, to the conflict of opinion, and an effort for increased and unusual effect, there is great danger that personal religion will be neglected, and the standard of personal piety will decline. The christian goes forth to the active duties of the day, not having suitably imbued his soul with the spirit of the gospel in his closet, and is therefore more exposed to indiscretions and mistakes. His ardour is not less glowing, his self-devotion not less entire, his laborious application to duty not less unremitted, but these fires may be "strange;" this self-sacrifice, ambitious; these labours, fanatical. In fine, there may be numbers, and energy, and disregard of ease and personal safety, and name; there may be a forgetfulness of every thing but the object, and, after all, it may prove to be another "crusade," prompted by ambition in some, fanaticism in others, sympathy in others, and fatal mistake in all. Had the blood and treasure expended, and the zeal, self-devotion, and labours bestowed in the crusades of the eleventh and twelfth centuries for rescuing Palestine from the hands of infidels, been prudently and piously employed to save infidels from unbelief and ruin; had the invasion of the Holy Land been bloodless, under the gospel commission, the conquest might now have been complete, and the triumph final. I here trace one of the principal dangers, which I perceive in the peculiar spirit and habits of the present age. The strong tendency to action, the desire for immediate effect, dictated, perhaps, by the best of feelings, by the love of souls, is hurrying men out from their retired meditations, fired with a "zeal not according to knowledge," not sufficiently chastened to accomplish great things "in the name of the Lord." I think I plainly see, in the "immediatism" of one class of christians of the present day, piety and zeal enough to subjugate the world, could it pervade the church universally, but indiscretion, and haste, and recklessness enough to ruin the christian cause, or retard it for centuries; all for want of the practical exercise and presiding influence of "that wisdom which cometh down from above, which is first pure, then peaceable, gentle, easy to be entreated, full of mercy and good fruits, without partiality and without hypocrisy." Unless this spirit be arrested, and a deeper spirit of humility pervade the church, I greatly fear her triumph is to be long deferred, and the bright sun of this day of hope will set in blood.

If I could do one thing for the church, and do but one, in the employment of means for her purification and efficient influence, I would shut up every member for one hour in his chamber for silent meditation, every morning before he goes forth to the business of the day. If I were called upon to name one indication more than any other of ill omen in the church at the present day, I should say there is a wildness in her eye, which indicates a want of suitable reflection. There is, indeed, a spirit-stirring influence now at work; there is a self-sacrificing spirit in the church, a zeal, an action, an energy, which would insure efficient results, if the mild, and humble, and unpretending spirit of "God as manifested in the flesh," is permitted to control and direct the whole. Oh, for the Spirit of Christ to pervade our spirits, to control, and mould, and energize the church on earth! Oh, for an unquenchable fire of devotion that may burn up our dross, and melt the church into one body! Oh, for the love that shone on Calvary, and the wisdom of God to temper and direct its energies! All this may be ours. And if it do not bless the church at large, it shall be the portion from the hand of God to each humble disciple, who waits in secret on him for direction. "Let the words of my mouth, and the meditation of my heart, be acceptable in thy sight, O Lord, my strength and my Redeemer."

## LETTER XXII.

### MEDITATION.

My dear Children,—Meditation is as necessary to form a consistent religious character as it is essential to a spirit of devotion. Our duty must be carefully examined, our object distinctly apprehended, our plans deliberately formed, our course of action premeditated and defined, and the whole frequently reviewed. Under painful experience of the world's influence on a spirit of devotion, the soul aspiring to a religious life may be disposed to abandon the connections, which furnish such fatal temptations. Thus originated, very early in the history of the church, the monastic life. In a contemplative mood, and smarting under the effects of temptation and sinful compliances, most serious persons have been led sometimes to desire seclusion from the world. Leaving this extreme, and engaging in the active duties of life, we are liable to be driven to an opposite error, and neglect retired meditation altogether. We are not at liberty to retire from active duty in society. A part of that duty therefore lies in a preparation for social and public life by retired private meditation.

We cannot understand all truth at once, nor the various important bearings of any one truth. We must be practised in the school of Christ, and we are learners in mental discipline, and in intellectual acquisition, as children introduced to a new circle of objects, or a new science. It is by reflection and study that we advance in religious knowledge. It comes not by intuition, nor does it appear in its maturity to the unpractised faculties of the soul. We first can only say that, whereas we were once blind, now we see. But our vision is imperfect. We see men as trees walking. We come gradually to greater distinctness of vision, and maturity of understanding. We arrive at clear views of truth only by serious, continued, and persevering meditation upon it.

But it is not only necessary that we be intellectual christians by admitting the evidence of the christian religion, and yielding our assent to its claims, but also that we be christians indeed by having our minds imbued with the spirit of the truth. This is one of the results of religious meditation on a mind, which has been touched and renewed by its power. To treasure the truth in memory's store-house, and call it up in the secret silence of the mind to occupy its leisure hours, and to give direction to its affections and energies, is a means of imparting to the soul the spirit of the truth itself. It is like leaven; when quickened and energized by divine grace in the heart, it diffuses itself, and imparts its own qualities to the whole mass.

It is the means and source of devotion. David says, "While I was musing, the fire burned." A spirit of holy devotion is awakened in the heart while it meditates on divine truth. The psalmist also breaks forth in the following rapturous exclamation, "Oh, how love I thy law; it is my meditation all the day!" What is the result? "I have," he says, "more understanding than all my teachers; for thy testimonies are my meditation." Again, he says—"How sweet are thy words unto my taste! yea, sweeter than honey to my mouth!" And again he declares, "My zeal hath consumed me"—"I delight to do thy will, O my God!" Thus his habit of retired meditation was, to David, the fruitful source of love, knowledge, happiness, and devotion. Yet he cultivated this habit, so efficient to control his conduct, amid the most numerous duties which pressed upon him as the ruler of a great people, and with a multitude of private duties rarely exceeded.

I separate meditation, as a religious exercise, from self-examination, to which I design to call your attention in my next. It may, and properly will, be connected with that self-examination and attended with secret prayer—but it is a separate and distinct exercise. The result of our self-examination may furnish a subject for meditation; so may any truth at any time. In mixed company, where no profitable subject is introduced, the mind that is contemplative may always abstract its own attention, and select its own subject. Where no rules of civility call for our particular attentions to the company, this may always be done with propriety, and sometimes with profit; as among strangers in a stage-coach or steamboat; where the conversation is engrossed by subjects and by persons with whom we cannot sympathize. The "mind is its own place," and should be so disciplined as not to be subjected to the control of every tongue that cannot be silent, and yet has no sense to utter.

I dislike to see a young lady always in a "brown study," or absent, without good reason, from the company she is in; but it sometimes is excellent to see a modest female really inattentive to impertinence, which was designed to engage her attention. You have heard the story of the "little red book." A female was travelling in a stage coach, with a mixed company—one of them a young man, loud with his infidelity. The lady was silent. She had a "little red book," containing pious meditations. She occasionally opened it, and pursued her own reflections. Soon they were involved in difficulty and danger, through the imprudence of an intoxicated driver. The infidel abandoned his argument. His cheek turned pale, his lip quivered. Now the lady sat unmoved and resigned. She continued her profitable and appropriate meditations, while the agitated infidel, disconcerted, was left to his principles with no habit of pious contemplation.

Profitable subjects of meditation are furnished everywhere in the common incidents of life. But the richest, the best, are contained in those precious portions of scripture which you have marked with your pencil and committed to memory. The promises, how precious as subjects of meditation! The love of God, the sufferings of Christ, the atonement, the blessed state and employments of heaven—subjects like these under a comprehensive text that embraces or leads to any one of them, may well engross the thoughts to the exclusion of all ordinary subjects.

While you should scrupulously avoid all affectation of a musing, contemplative mood, and likewise all reality of an absent manner in company, never hesitate to think, and to think independently, for yourselves. I know it is a terrible idea to some men to be in the society of a thinking lady. Those are the very beings whom I would have you to repel from your company. The gospel gives you the rights, and subjects you to the responsibility, of reasonable, intelligent, and accountable beings. Act worthy of your true dignity, and bind that gospel to your hearts which has rescued your sex from the control of those monsters in the shape of men, who are afraid to see the signs of intellectual development in a lady. You are always their superiors, and can, and ought to, subject them to their merited obscurity. I once saw one of them struck perfectly dumb for the remainder of the journey, to the great relief of the whole company in a stage coach, by the sprightly and intelligent reply of a young lady, whom he sought to engage in conversation without sense. He attempted to rally her from a pensive mood by the best remark he had yet made, in that little borrowed sentence, "A penny for your thoughts." "I have been admiring," said she, "these noble hills of granite—pray, sir, what are the minerals of your State?" What he meant, perhaps, as a jest, proved a reality—she had thoughts, and he had none.

## LETTER XXIII.

### SELF-EXAMINATION AND SECRET PRAYER.

My dear Children,—Daily devotion, of which I have been urging you to form right habits, embraces self-examination and secret prayer, in connection with reading the Bible, and meditation. I need not say that individual character, in its public display to others in the common intercourse of life, will depend on the fidelity with which these habits are cherished. They serve to revive and strengthen the principle of religion in the soul, if it has, by divine grace, been implanted there. They fan the flame of devotion, and trim the lamp, that its light may be clear and productive of practical good to all who are in the house.

In secret prayer, we come with the single and unembarrassed expression of our own feelings, always more or less constrained where we pray in the presence of others, or are led by their petitions. Social prayer is delightful, useful, necessary; but it can never supersede the necessity of those separate appeals, in which the soul comes with "its own bitterness," often of a private nature, and sometimes inexpressible, and pours out itself, in the strong and undissembled sorrows of a child, before Him who looketh on the heart. The affairs of the soul are of such a nature that they can never be settled, never disposed of in the gross. Its sins must be separately and minutely considered. Repentance must extend, separately and minutely, to our sins, or they will never be safely disposed of against the judgment day. This is not a concern in which we can throw ourselves on the plan of mercy in a great partnership with a world of sinners, and find our share of its benefits. These benefits come in exact accordance with the separate adaptations of the soul itself; and with every one, it is an individual concern, in which, as a convicted sinner, he is separately concerned, and answers for himself alone and entirely, just as if there were no other sinner in the universe.

We are exceedingly prone to find leaning places, to rest on others, and to involve ourselves, so as to throw off personal responsibility. This is always dangerous—it is fatal just so far as it involves deadly sins. We cannot transfer responsibility. You must answer for yourselves; and even a parent on whom you are accustomed to lean, to whom you look for advice, who takes you up and cherishes you, and often assumes your cares, cannot come to your relief in this great matter. You must, then, know yourselves. You must come to Christ separately and alone. You must stand in judgment at the bar of your own consciences, and before God, at an audience where I cannot enter, where no human footstep can intrude, where angels cannot be admitted.

The root of all guilt is deep laid in the human constitution; it germinates and shows its living principle in the strong and secret workings of the heart; it brings forth its fruit in the public acts, seen and known of all men. But the essential character of the tree is not radically changed when it brings no fruit to perfection; nor is the soul, rancorous in its hatred to God, less guilty because its bitterness is not developed by external acts to the observation of others. Between the soul and God, then, there lies a great, solemn, and personal matter of concern, which requires an individual and separate examination, interview, and reconciliation at the throne of grace.

This view is of the most momentous importance. Many think religion consists in a public form; that they are religious when they condescend to read their Bible, say their prayers, sanction the Sabbath and public preaching by their presence, receive baptism, and partake of the Lord's supper, as sealing ordinances, the former constituting regeneration, and the latter communion with God. So far from it, these holy sacraments, thus perverted, become the seal of their damnation. They condemn themselves in what they do. They eat and drink damnation to themselves. True religion lies between the soul and God. It has been excluded by a spirit of enmity—that enmity must be slain. It may be dishonoured by worldly compliances—all those cherished habits must be abandoned. Love to God, and devotion to his cause, as a living principle in the heart, must lay the foundation for all our professions, hopes, and peace in believing. Daily communion with God, sweet, near and personal, must prove to us the reality of our religion, and be the life of our hope.

To know what we are in religion, then, we must keep a separate, personal account with ourselves. We must go separately to God with our case. We must, in the secret silence of the mind, examine ourselves in regard to the spirit and temper we cherish, in relation to God, to our neighbour, to every object with which we are connected, or to which we are related. Without this we can never know what manner of spirit we are of. We can never go to God, carrying our wants and ordering our speech aright. With the knowledge we have acquired, we can carry our case before the throne. We can present precisely the point that labours. We can go with it to the

Bible, and there learn what is its character as tried by the law. We can go with it before a throne of grace, and ask of God, for Christ's sake, the very mercy we need; and then we may be able to know the results. With this knowledge of our true standing, we shall be able to apply to ourselves the consolations or alarms which the truth in the case may warrant.

Self-examination is absolutely necessary to a knowledge of ourselves. Secret prayer, in which we go alone to God, is equally necessary to lead us to this definite knowledge, and to cherish it in our bosoms. These positions are proved in the experience of all christians. We cannot live a day but they are fully verified, and the longer we live the more deeply will our experience enforce them on our conviction.

The time to be occupied in private devotion, embracing self-examination and prayer, must be, to some extent, subject to circumstances, and cannot be prescribed with any uniform rule of universal application. It must, in all cases, however, be daily practised, if possible. It is not safe to let the events of a single day pass into the undistinguished history of the past, without review; to let one unrepented sin pass into forgetfulness, to rise up fresh in our vivid recollection at the day of judgment. The morning and evening are seasons naturally marked and suited to these duties, and they should be both improved, if possible, to furnish an hour, at least, for private devotion. This is not always practicable; and when it is not, the mind ought to avail itself of its habit of meditation, to retire even in the midst of company, to compose itself to a devotional frame, to put on the armour suited to its warfare, and to recognize and feel its personal responsibilities. "The little red book" may be extracted from the indispensable as an essential article of its furniture, a subject out of it for the morning or evening furnished, and replaced without so much disrespect to your fellow worms, as you would show disrespect to God by a neglect to raise your heart in prayer and praise at the beginning or close of the day. But, in ordinary circumstances, we may find set forms of retirement practicable, of greater or less duration. When we rise in the morning, it is always convenient to bend the knee at our bedside, and make the discipline and religious exercise of the soul a part of the ceremony of dressing. The same may be said of our hour and forms of retiring to rest.

Observe the habits of pious men and women, as disclosed in their memoirs, where those records have admitted us to a view of their retired habits of devotion and self-discipline. Observe, in your own experience, what is necessary to your spiritual life and enjoyment, and practise accordingly. Col. Gardiner, amid the trials and tumults of the camp, uniformly rose two hours before day, that he might employ those silent and undisturbed hours in private devotion. The habits of Sir Matthew Hale were similar. Sir Edward Coke, another eminent English jurist, expressed his views in the following couplet:

> " Six hours in sleep, in law's grave study six,
> Four spend in prayer, the rest on nature fix."

Sir William Jones says:

> " Six hours to law, to soothing slumber seven,
> Ten to the world allot, and all to heaven."

## LETTER XXIV.

### THE RESULT OF A HOLY LIFE.

My dear Children,—As much as my widowed heart embraces you, the living images of your departed mother; and as much as I depend on you to take her place in my earthly affections, so far as those affections can be transferred, or you can occupy a larger space in a father's love, I would yet much rather see you die prepared, and live a while alone, in the hope of an eternal union, than to enjoy your society to old age here, with the prospect of an eternal separation. It is now with the hope that in one of various ways I may bring *death* to your view in an impressive form, connected with the results of a holy life, I give you some further particulars of a young lady already referred to, in my thirteenth letter, under the name of Sophronia. The following is the close of the sermon preached at her funeral, Feb. 28, 1825.

"Sophronia Coleman* was born January 19, 1802, and, of course, died near the age of twenty-three. As far as personal beauty is valuable, she

* Daughter of Dr. William Coleman, of Pittsfield, Mass.

was sufficiently favoured by nature. She possessed a mind active, strong, and discriminating. Under favourable advantages, she cultivated her intellectual powers so far as to place her in a rank with the most accomplished of her sex. The chief excellence of her character, however, and that which it is most pleasant to hear and speak of at her funeral, is that the 'Lord was her hope,' Although myself a stranger to her early years, I speak with confidence when I say, the birth of this hope in her childhood was attended with that conviction of sin, that penitence, that fleeing to Christ, that trust in him, that joy, those good fruits which are characteristic of the true christian. That it was operative, and supported her in the near prospect of death, is also eminently true.

"Another most interesting fact in her history is, that 'God was her hope, even from her youth.' At the age of seven years, she became the subject of serious impressions, and at that early period of life, after a course of very distressing conviction, she commenced the discharge of christian duties, under which her hope has been strengthened, and she was richly furnished for the final conflict to which she has been so early, not to say prematurely, called. From this early age, she exhibited a decided change in her general deportment, and commenced those retired religious duties which will ever characterize a fervent spirit. It is interesting to learn from those who were the observers of her daily walk that, at this early age, she commenced the duty of secret prayer, and there is evidence that the duty has never been omitted for a single day since that time when she was able to retire.

"Her uniform habit was to retire for this purpose, three times a day—sometimes oftener. Her Bible and her closet were her delight. Indeed it is pleasant to notice in her pocket Bible, the evidence of good usage, and the many striking passages marked by her hand, to form the particular subjects of her meditation, and which have refreshed the soul of this lovely saint while on earth.

"Besides her regular attendance on her stated hours of prayer, she rarely undertook anything, not even the writing of a common letter, without first retiring to seek the blessing of God; and the space of one hour at her stated devotions, bore testimony that it was an employment she loved. I may add also, that the ear into which children, in their filial confidence, speak all they feel, has heard her often declare that she was sometimes constrained to spend whole nights in prayer, and that she often had the most delightful views of God and of divine truth.

"A spirit thus tender and thus imbued, it may be justly supposed, was very scrupulous in the regular discharge of every duty of life. It was so. Everything was ordered and arranged by her in reference to eternity, and a childhood and youth thus spent, could not but bring forward old age with rapidity, if we 'count that life long, which answers life's great end.' She is now gone —gone for ever! But she lived long enough She was older than many of more numerous years. It is pleasant to be able to say such things at her funeral, it brings consolation to mourners, and instruction to all. Let it speak. Let it speak to youth—especially to those of her own sex.

" First, consider the early age at which she commenced a religious life, and hear the manner in which she speaks of the beginning of life as favourable for religious duty and enjoyment. What I am about to repeat is from a very creditable piece, which, from among a great mass of her manuscripts, found its way into a periodical paper. 'The morning of life,' says she, 'is altogether the most favourable season for a life of holiness, as the heart is more tender and more susceptible of religious impressions. Should any misguided youth flatter himself that a few dying confessions will atone for his sins, and appease the wrath of an incensed God, he will, in horror and despair, find himself awfully mistaken, and with bitter experience and lamentation, feel the justice of God in withholding then that mercy, which he now so impiously disregards.'

"After such a commencement of her life, consider how she spent her time. Her Bible and her closet were her delight. They had charms which always could call her away from any pursuit of mere worldly pleasure. She was not melancholy—no one farther from it. Yet she was not vain, light, frivolous. She could smile at what was innocently gay or amusing, but she could not laugh at what was sinful. She did not shun society—she often enjoyed it. But all her social intercourse must be made subservient to her religious duties, or give way to them. She could not barter the happiness she found in her closet communing with her Saviour, for any other pleasures. She would not compromise on any matter which was to rob her of her devotions. She was not inattentive to her dress, for the most perfect neatness uniformly marked her person, and all that pertained to her. Neither was she unmindful of the common notices of civility in social life, for the discharge of which her religious habits eminently prepared her. But there was a mark of civility—something more—an imperious duty she owed her own soul and her Saviour, the paramount claim of which she ever felt, and on which she regulated her own conduct.

"Consider the end for which this course of life prepared her. When she saw death approaching with rapid and certain step, her steady eye looked on with composure. She was resigned—she was willing to die. She felt what those who think most seriously, feel most deeply, that it is a solemn thing to exchange worlds. Yet she trusted in God, and believed he had prepared for her a mansion in heaven. Under a state of nervous irritability, which attended her sickness, she did sometimes look on the pangs of death with dread; but God was very gracious to spare her this bitter experience, for I saw her gently sink into the arms of death with less apparent pain than it ordinarily cost her to breathe. So may we be permitted to fall asleep in death—not so much without a momentary struggle, as supported by a hope, and adorned with a character like hers.

"Finally, I ask you to consider, what would be your state, if this were your funeral instead of hers? Where would you be—in heaven, or hell? What variations must there have been in this discourse, to have suited your case? What kind of consolations should we have offered to surviving friends? The time will soon arrive, when the undertaker will be called to provide your funeral, when the solitary shroud shall take the place of your present coverings, when the tolling bell shall assemble your mourners, and when I shall be asked, if permitted to survive you, and to attend at your death-bed, how you felt, and how you died. Gay youth, where are you going in your vanity?

Stop, I entreat you. Consider well the consequences of what you do. And despise not, I beseech you, the forbearance of God, which would lead you to repentance.

"If there be any condition to be envied, it is that of a pious youth brought to an early grave. He has lived long enough to reap all that can be here gained. He has 'answered life's great end.' He has ripened for a higher state of being and enjoyment, and he has nothing that should detain him here. The cares of this life, in its best enjoyment, must press heavily upon him. But everything in his life in heaven is bright and pure.

"How sweet is the sleep of a saint in death! How dignified! How glorious his resurrection! How interesting the associations which attend on his funeral, solemn, sublime, glorious! Such let mine be. Such be yours. 'Let me die the death of the righteous, and let my last end be like his.' But to die the death of the righteous, we must have his hope, we must live his life, we must possess his experience. Are you destitute of this hope, this life, this experience? Just answer this question. Answer it before God, and at the tribunal of conscience. Answer it at the grave's mouth to-day, and on the brink of eternity. Then, let your future life be regulated by the answer. For soon the prospect before you will be past over, the name you so carefully trace on every object you here possess, and call it yours, will be obliterated. Instead of the pleasure it now imparts, its very sound will awaken melancholy recollections in the minds of surviving friends. It will be transferred from other places and stand solitary, engraved on the marble slab that marks your grave. Soon the marble crumbles, and no place is found on earth to recover your history. The earth itself shall be burnt up, while it is proclaimed through the universe—'Time shall be no longer.' And is this all? No. Before these things, the earth and sea shall give up their dead, and you shall live, deathless, immortal, quick to feel your moral obligation, which can never cease to hold you to the law of God; and alive to experience, through eternity, all that, for which your earthly probation, then finished, shall have prepared you."

## LETTER XXV.

### PHYSICAL EDUCATION.

My dear Children,—Religion prepares us to live in the best manner, and possesses a vital principle, which death cannot reach. At death, "tongues shall cease and knowledge shall vanish away;" "sin kills beyond the tomb," but "charity never faileth." It is not without a reason, therefore, that I have said so much, and dwelt so long on the formation of religious character and habits. Review what I have said, and carefully reduce to practice a father's counsels, drawn from the word of God, sanctioned by experience, and enforced by every filial obligation, by every principle of duty.

Although flesh is dust, and is soon turned to corruption, yet it forms a tenement for the immortal spirit here, and acts with great power on our moral and intellectual constitution. It deserves, therefore, the most careful attention, much more than is commonly awarded to it. If we compare our bodies with all other works of art, whether in nature, or in the sphere of human ingenuity, we shall be struck with its superior mechanical perfection, beauty, and utility. It is ours—furnished and fitted to the uses of the soul by a divine architect. If we attend to the anatomy of its structure, every minute and separate part surprises us by its curious workmanship and acurate adaptations. The eye, how wonderfully delicate in its structure, commodious in the position assigned to it, and how signally various and important its uses! Put it out, and we are left in perpetual midnight. And yet, always waking, we are soon wearied, and languish for want of rest. How wonderful the provision, which enables the body, by the dictate of its own weariness, to wrap this globe of light with its lenses and picture-canvass, in a fold of its own flesh, so that its exciting causes cease, and the world is shut out from the soul, left to rest, or to its own meditations! Preserve carefully that delicate organ, so necessary to the student, so important whether we pursue business, or amusement, or pleasure, so indispensable in everything. By inattention to this caution, so common with the young, we are often called to see the incongruity of youth in spectacles; parents are disappointed of their hopes in the education of their children, compelled to relinquish their studies, and premature old age seizes on the most sensitive and important inlet of knowledge and thought.

Similar remarks might be made in application to all the senses, which would impress upon us the duty to preserve them unimpaired, and direct them on objects which might contribute to our pleasure, constantly sustained without an unnecessary expenditure of animal life. The mind should be also awakened to similar reflections on all the parts and powers of our physical constitution. The hand and arm, how admirably adapted in all their powers of motion for the uses to which they are designed! We cannot lose a finger nail, without serious injury. We cannot improve in a single particular on the wisdom of God.

I have no doubt that in the philosophy of nature's works, we shall find that utility adds essentially to the beauty of objects. There is a great mistake in the estimates commonly formed of personal beauty, as consisting in lines, surfaces, and colours. Unconnected with utility no forms can continue to please. On the contrary, objects the most pleasing soon change even to disgust. This is universally true, even of personal charms. Matrimonial connections, therefore, which are formed on mere fancy, where there are no enduring qualities to command respect, usually terminate unhappily, and for the plain reason that "beauty soon fades." The qualities of the mind and heart alone survive to exert their abiding influence on the respect and love of the admirers of our gayer and fresher days.

Ordinarily, the greatest calamity, which can befall a young lady, is to be pronounced by the world beautiful in her person. Like other animal substances, which attract merely sensual flies and insects, she is soon surrounded by a swarm of creatures which blight all that is fair, and turn to disease all that is healthful and sound. The moment a young lady is pronounced a beauty, there is an end to study and the cultivation of more enduring qualities. Soon, she has no time for anything but dress, and balls, and parties, and idle conversation with the idle. The breath of flattery has reached her, and she is inflated, giddy, and light. I have never seen an unfortunate being of this class, who was contented with the "form and feature" that nature had given her. She must needs have "some improvement still." And health is soon undermined by the corset, the light dress, and exposure to night air. A little disappointment or chagrin is sufficient to send the vital current rushing to the heart, to engorge the lungs already compressed and dislodged from the ample space which nature assigned them, and she sinks to an early grave in a quick consumption. But if she survives these repeated shocks and physical obstructions, nature relaxes and gradually sinks. The fading cheek must be renewed by artificial touches of the pencil, new teeth must be stolen from the dead, the breath must be perfumed, tresses borrowed, and soon a form, almost entirely artificial, stands the object of general neglect, where lately that beauty shone and attracted the gaze of fools. The beauty has vanished into the air, and there is nothing left to interest the beholder.

The greatest physical blessing is health, and a form without personal beauty; completeness in all the limbs and organs without deformity. When measured in all its dangers and ordinary influence, it is undoubtedly a greater calamity to be beautiful, than to be deformed, as much as humility is better than pride. With a judicious constitution of habits, health is preserved, and personal improvements come with age, while youthful beauty is often lavished or murdered by the very artificial means used to increase it.

The preservation of health is among our first duties, and inseparable from the first law of nature which requires us to preserve our lives. Intimately dependent on it are happiness and useful ness, as well as moral soundness and intellectual vigour. On the subject of health, let me say to you, it is principally affected by three causes—employment, diet, and exercise.

Employment, both of body and of mind, is essential to sound health. This is the order of nature, the law of God. This employment should suitably fill up our time, and be fitted in its degree to our strength, and peculiar circumstances. The mere lounging student will never be characterized by an active and energetic intellect. You cannot acquire your lesson in bed any better than you can sew or knit there. The mind insists on a posture suited to the body. Even in his studies, the student should maintain an erect posture, especially at the writing-table, that the chest may be thrown open, and the lungs have their proper room. The apparel should be suitably loose to allow the regular circulations unobstructed, and nature should, in all things, be allowed to proceed without interruptions. The decencies and proprieties of life are the forms and manners, which the scholar should carry into the duties of the school, and the school-room. The mind should find its employment in study as a matter of business. It should be occupied with the subject until it is mastered, revived by suitable relaxation, but never suffered to wander in airy speculations, or waste its energy in an idle, lazy habit. A too intense application, long continued, may prove as fatal as lassitude and laziness.

The diet of a student should always be plain, moderate, and seasonable. The luxurious table is unsuited to the promotion of health and happiness under all circumstances—but fatal to those of a sedentary and studious habit. Many of the peculiar diseases of students, I have observed, have their origin in a want of care in eating, either too much or too little, of improper food, or at unsuitable seasons.

But the evils from the two sources just mentioned would be much diminished by a proper regard to exercise and rest. To a student it is of great importance these should be regular, and suitable both in kind and quantity. The vigour, both of body and mind, depends greatly on a quietude and equilibrium, to which due exercise and rest are essentially requisite. Early rising, and early rest, are very judiciously made a subject of law in your school. But every one requires a personal discipline, to make the best rules available to the greatest good. I will now only say, let not a busy and anxious mind interrupt and dissipate your appropriate hours of rest. Discipline and curb a prurient imagination. Require the mind, when you lie down, to relinquish both its work and its play. Suppress anxiety, that you may invite sleep, "kind nature's sweet restorer." Rise when you wake, if it be the hour for rising. Never indulge in a slothful disposition in bed. Relax the mind from all its efforts in the hours of recreation, and apply it with undivided attention when engaged, and let your exercise be always sufficient to save the mind from lassitude and fatigue in its regular duties of study. In this way every change becomes a source of relaxation, and the mind, necessarily active, finds its enjoyments in its duties.

So far as physical endowments are considered, the young lady who enjoys good health and a proper person, and preserves them, will soon surpass, in all that has power to please, the acknowledged beauty who passes her summer day in the sunshine of flattery that is rendered to the "fading forms" and dying colours of flesh and blood. Your early friends will soon be greatly diminished in number, by change of circumstances, if not by death. Flatterers, if you have been so unfortunate as to have them, will seek new objects of admiration and attention, and you will find yourselves left to the circles of moral or intellectual society, which you have secured by the stern habits of your own minds, or to the few friends whose attachment you have secured by the unfailing exercise of those habits and virtues.

## LETTER XXVI.

### DEPORTMENT TOWARDS TEACHERS.

My dear Children,—When I commit your education to other hands, I of necessity relinquish my personal supervision and attention. Could I abandon you in the most important and critical period of your life to your own inexperience, or to the influence of bad counsels or bad examples, I should betray my highest trust to do it. I require in your teachers not only ability to teach, but authority and moral energy to govern. I require a character, which you can respect, and a sense of responsibility, which will make that government parental. I do not say that all teachers of youth possess these qualifications, but none others could receive my patronage, none others should receive any patronage.

I would no sooner commit the instruction of my child to one, in whose whole character I could not have entire confidence, than I would place pure gold in the hands of a dishonest goldsmith to set my jewels, or expose those jewels, unprotected, to thieves and robbers. These views of my own responsibility have dictated my duties toward you in providing for your education.

The parent, who can place his child beyond his supervision without subjection to a competent authority, and a safe protection, has never yet learnt the true responsibility, nor felt the proper sympathy of a parent. The teacher who cannot himself feel the responsibility of a parent, and who is not awakened to all the deep sympathies of a parent, is unfit to conduct the education of the young. The youth, who does not regard his teacher with something of that respect which is due to a parent, with the subjection rendered to a protector, is not prepared to profit suitably by his instructions, will neither make a profitable scholar, nor a grateful child.

Respect is not the subject of command. It must be the deliberate and free assent of the mind to acknowledged worth. The deserving teacher secures it from his pupil, and if he cannot, he is unfit to teach. Doing this, he will generally gain willingly, that which must be enforced if necessary—obedience. The parent who does not enforce this upon his child, and demand it in the government of the school, indulges his child to his own ruin. There is not a deeper root of evil, that a parent can plant in the path of a youth, than to commit his education to unskilful hands, or inculcate such sentiments as will lead him to insubordination, or encourage and support him in disobedience to the rules of the school. In the school-room, and the period of pupilage, character is taking its cast. The mind is thrown into the mould, and is passing as from a state of fusion to a permanent form. This it is, which gives to this period of life and to these circumstances, their principal power over our future destinies. Here is the secret of that influence which the teacher must exert over his pupil for weal or for wo.

The youth who receives lessons of insubordination under parental sanction, will be lawless under every government in after life. He will be a bad citizen, a bad husband, a bad neighbour, a bad parent, bad in every relation. An unruled spirit prepares for rebellion to every rightful authority, and will hurry its possessor on to war with the Most High. The same spirit will make a tyrant in the exercise of authority, and will subject every action to the control of caprice or passion. The school-rooms, therefore, may be regarded as the little nurseries of the commonwealth, where its meritorious sons and daughters, its good citizens, its devoted mothers, are trained to their duties, and prepared to bless their country.

I respect, therefore, the laborious, devoted, and successful teacher of youth. If any citizen deserves distinguished honour of his country, it is the man, who has spent a long and laborious life in the successful education of her citizens, her sons and her daughters, become at length the fathers and mothers of a new generation. I make these remarks to you, my children, to present distinctly to your view the principle on which you owe respect and obedience to your teachers. Rightly understood, the principle will produce a right practice as the spontaneous action of your own conviction and choice. But as I have ever required obedience of my children at home, I require it on the grounds already stated, at school—obedience to those to whom I have committed their education. It is not for the pupil to resist the laws of the school. You have an appeal to me, and I may support you, and always will support you against tyrannical or unjust inflictions. But the remedy is removal not rebellion. I am with you in a permission to retire from the operation of severe or oppressive laws, but not in resisting them. We live under a government of civil laws, which protect every citizen from oppression. The organization of a school is, under those laws, incapable of invading the essential rights of the weakest child. This is enough for protection. If we abandon that protection and allow every child to decide for herself what is right, we relinquish our wholesome laws, and return to anarchy. When the co-operation of the parent, in support of the authority exercised over youth at school, is withdrawn, our academies and colleges will but cherish and mature that spirit, which has ever been the sworn enemy of liberty, and which indulged, always will march, as it ever has marched, through anarchy to despotism.

A teacher may indeed be oppressive and wrong. His conduct may be outrageous and insufferable. But a good teacher will never be so. If parents will employ drunken or unprincipled masters, they must take the consequences, the ruin of their children, and the subversion of law. But the fault is their own. The evil commences from the root, and is inseparable from the character of the men whom they patronize, perhaps to gain a penny, or to gratify a whim. I reason, however, from different premises. I have confidence in your teachers. They, of course, are entitled to your respect, and secure it. They require obedience, and have my co-operation in its enforcement. Under these premises, if the student resist authority, the presumption is always against him, and it devolves on him to make out his case.

Let me say to you, ever seek to gain the confidence and good opinion of your teachers; not by servile compliances, but by a strict and conscientious attention to duty. Avoid servility in your bearing towards every one, and never seek a familiarity with your superiors by making yourselves useful as tale-bearers. Avoid the character of an informer, and avoid those who sustain it. In their zeal to serve their superiors, and gain their reward, they usually become liars, and mean in every sentiment of the soul. Never hesitate, on the other hand, to tell the truth when questioned by proper authority, though it expose a friend, though it expose yourselves. Never tell a lie, never equivocate, never conceal yourselves by unworthy means, nor aid to conceal others from the just operation of the law. Do nothing wrong, and, if possible, be privy to nothing wrong in others. But when called to give testimony, tell the truth. Let all understand from your known character, that you are not spies upon your companions; and let them know, also, that if they commit wrong under your cognizance, you are not the wretches that will equivocate and wrong yourselves, to save them from merited punishment or disgrace.

## LETTER XXVII.

### FORMATION OF FRIENDSHIPS.

MY DEAR CHILDREN,—The influence exerted on the character of youth by the intercourse they hold with their companions, and the habits they here form, is too important and vital to be disposed of in a single paragraph. I wish now to direct your attention distinctly to it that you may be placed on your guard against insidious evils, and derive every advantage from this intercourse, which it offers to the mind studious of self-improvement.

The boarding-school furnishes many advantages, which are peculiar to its organization, and which should be improved by you diligently, while the concomitant evils are carefully avoided. Such a school is commonly regarded as select, and in some respects it is. But the selection is by no means in strict and single reference to points, which render the selection always best suited to your companionship. It unfortunately happens that the best family government and the purest lessons of morality are not always inculcated in those families, which are most privileged, and among those who are able to select the highest schools for the education of their children. Hence, you must sometimes encounter bad examples from high sources. You may find, even in young ladies of parentage highly respectable, maxims and views of propriety, examples and habits, which you have been taught to avoid; often a disregard of religion, and even sometimes infidel sentiments. The allowed and allowable habits of the different classes of society, are sometimes found assembled together in the same boarding-school, and without reflection and a proper discrimination, you may greatly err by confounding things that should be separated, or by condemning in others what is suited to their circumstances, although it might be improper and wrong in yours.

The first advice I shall give you, will regard the selection of your confidential friends. Let them be few and wisely chosen. They are your familiar associates, and will necessarily bring into your society, and urge on your approbation, all their peculiar views, habits and sentiments. In the selection of these friends, have a principal reference to the qualities of the heart and the head. You cannot sweetly commune and walk together, unless there be "thought, feeling, taste, harmonious with your own." With this communion life is twice enjoyed. We are happy in ourselves, and happy in our friends' happiness.

Having selected your friends, do not feel that a real confidence requires you to adopt all their habits and opinions, or to surrender your own This is servility. You may have found a friend in one, whose circumstances in life are very different from your own. It is not necessary to all the benefits of that friendship that you should regulate your habits of life and expenditure by hers. These differences are trifling, and should be but little thought of. Especially should you resist a disposition to conform, where the change would require you to increase your expenditure, perhaps, beyond your ability, and involve you in serious evils.

When you have deliberately admitted one to your friendship, give her your confidence. Friendship is otherwise worth nothing, it is nothing. Let that confidence, deliberately extended, not be slightly withdrawn. If distrust find a place in your feelings, seek an explanation. There may be some mistake, an enemy may have sown tares, or your friend may be trying your sincerity. Never withdraw your confidence, once given, but on clear evidence that it has been abused. On that evidence withdraw it promptly and professedly.

Never desert your friend because deserted by

others. Then prove your friendship, when she is in misfortune. Defend her good name from the slander of evil tongues, and let no one, let no combination of numbers or of influence, separate you from your friends, where no personal dereliction has forfeited your confidence. Prosperity extends the circle of friends; adversity proves the true, and therefore, reduces it to narrow limits. These only are worthy the name.

But while you extend your confidence and intimacy to few, let all share your attention and complaisance. None are to be neglected and avoided, unless crime has shut them out from our communion. Even this should not debar them from our sympathy. Avoid that exclusive manner, which prevents a complaisant deportment toward all but your particular friends. Remember you were made for society, and a just regard to the rights of others will conciliate the respect and good will of all.

Cherish no enmities. If you have enemies, take care not to reciprocate their hatred. It is not necessary that you should force your good offices upon them. Put not yourselves in their power, but "love your enemies, bless them that curse you, do good to them that hate you, pray for them which despitefully use you and persecute you." The beautiful and forcible argument, by which the Saviour urged the cultivation of this amiable temper, may be found in his Sermon on the Mount. "That ye may be," said he, "the children of your Father, who is in heaven; for he maketh his sun to rise on the evil and on the good, and sendeth his rain on the just and on the unjust."

The heart, which cherishes these sentiments, cannot be easily disturbed by the enmities that rankle in other bosoms. Do what is right, and you will ever stand on a proud pre-eminence above those, who may seek to hurt you. Entertain no enmities. Wish ill to no one. If others indulge these feelings they are the only sufferers. They cannot essentially injure you.

Exercise a forgiving temper. You are not obliged to embrace your enemies. But if they confess their wrong forgive them; yet be cautious not to place yourselves in their power. Sometimes an ingenuous mind may do you an injury. When convinced of that, let a suitable reparation secure your confidence.

Seek to discriminate wisely in judging of character; not with affectation—that is the mark of a little mind. Experience will soon enable a diligent observer to distinguish the great outlines of character on a slight acquaintance. They are derived more accurately from the conversation and deportment, than from any peculiar conformation of the cranium or physiognomy.

In the large circle of acquaintances made in youth at a public school, a foundation may be laid for lasting benefits in future life. These hundreds of young persons, with whom you now associate, are soon to be scattered over a wide extent of country. They will form new connections, and enter on the duties of mature age in spheres of influence and responsibility. The associations of early life will often be renewed, and the hold you now take on them will remain unbroken by time and distance. These early friendships will be lasting as life, and not only where intimacies have been formed. You make and sustain a character in the society of your companions. That character stands in their minds just as it existed when you were separated at the close of your academic course. A great variety of incidents may transpire in life to make that character important to you. Here you may be laying a foundation for many years. Let every act be dictated under a conviction that you are making a character which is to last as long as you live, which is to stand before a wide extent of country, and sustain or injure you, to secure you respect, or place you in low estimation, before a wide circle of society. Those of you who live will soon meet each other as ladies in the common, various, and high relations of life. What you will desire then to be in the estimation of others, you now have an opportunity to make yourselves.

It is the lamentable mistake of many that they suppose one set of rules is to regulate propriety of manners, and even morality of action among youth, and another and severer rule to apply to mature age. Mature age is the childhood of our true existence, as early life is the childhood of riper years. Over all is spread the same universal rule of moral right, the same government of God. To him we are amenable from the infancy of our being, and shall be compelled to answer to that law, which requires truth in the inward parts, and holiness.

The intercourse of youth, then, to be truly profitable, must be religious, regulated by the same laws which govern the universe of intelligent beings, unvaried in their nature, and strict in their application.

Always prefer those for your intimate companionship, who give evidence that they are influenced by religious principle. True piety is not absolutely necessary to form an agreeable companion, or a true friend; yet personal religion, wherever it exists, establishes and regulates the moral integrity, and is the only sure safeguard of virtue. The crowning excellence of a friend then must be the principle of religion in the heart.

Finally, never seek by servile compliances either to gain a friend or conciliate an enemy.

Feel and do what is right. Seek first your own approbation, the approbation of an enlightened conscience, and never forget that to preserve your own self-respect you must incur the displeasure of some others. If you lose the approbation of others in the discharge of duty, you will gain more than you lose. "If ye suffer for righteousness' sake, blessed are ye"—says divine inspiration. There is the blessing, in suffering for doing that which is right. The friends you gain by this course, hold in high estimation. All others you can better spare than retain.

## LETTER XXVIII.

### THE VIRTUE OF ECONOMY.

MY DEAR CHILDREN,—The expenses of youth in a course of education are necessarily great, and, in most cases, impose a material burthen upon parents, especially if there are several to be educated in the same family. A dutiful and thoughtful child will not be inconsiderate on this subject.

It must be confessed that the young are not alone to blame for the extravagant habits into which our youth of both sexes are rapidly plunging, and which are calculated, in all their protracted consequences, to prejudice, in every important respect, the cause of education. Parents, in these defaults, are often more guilty than their children. Means of luxury and dissipation are often furnished for the vain parade of wealth. To show off above others has been the cherished pride of the parent, and is inculcated by example, and every facility furnished to their heirs apparent. To say nothing of the general evil of such an example, an evil which makes their wealth a curse to the community, it becomes, in this way, a curse to themselves, corrupting the fountains of moral, as well as animal life, and usually wastes the largest estates in the course of two or three generations. It is from causes of this kind, more than any other, that property is continually changing hands, and revolutions are going on, which reduce the rich to poverty, and raise the provident poor to wealth.

The evils of these habits indulged are manifold and most pernicious. Once contracted, they are not easily abandoned. They must be fed at a great and increasing expense. If, as is sometimes the case, the parent is not ruined in his pecuniary fortune by the education of his children, a foundation is laid for that ruin to follow rapidly after his death.

The example thus set by those who are able to support their extravagance is contagious. Others less able ape the pernicious practice, and incalculable evils follow.

Then, there is the influence exerted on the health and moral principle of the youth at the time. An indulgence in luxury or dissipation saps the foundation of health. Extravagance in dress and personal decorations, in fashion and public display, cherishes a frivolous and giddy turn of mind, to the exclusion of all sober and profitable thought. There is no room left for serious reflection, or the close application of the rules of duty; religion is rejected as an intruder, and moral principle cannot abide the issue.

The influence on the great objects of education is blighting and fatal. The attention is diverted from its appropriate objects. Study is neglected. Intellectual attainment is out of the question, and the scholar is lost in the fashionable young lady. She admires herself, is perhaps admired by a few others, has her day and dies.

Besides the immediate defeat of the great objects of education, which is thus suffered, the lasting effect on mental discipline prepares for more lasting evils, disappointment and chagrin. I have seen this disappointment paint the image of a mortified spirit on the countenance of the gay young lady, even before she has left the boarding school, or finished her education. All her expedients for multiplying and giving effect to her attractions are artificial. They sometimes fail, and the effect is, with every repetition, diminished. On the other hand, the permanent and unadorned excellences of thought, and of the countenance speaking those thoughts in its simple, natural, and eloquent expressions, are constantly improving with an educated intellect. While the former, therefore, is wasting and waning, the latter glows with a purer light, and burns with a brighter flame. The attractions of dress and fashion lose their power, while the bright sun of intellect and sparkling wit hold the attention and gain permanent approbation. Mind gives the principal beauty to the human form above other animals. By this crowning glory, it excels even the beauty of the peacock or the glow-worm; it surpasses the marble statue, and mocks the skill of the painter's pencil. So the human countenance, animated and expressing the glory of an enlightened intellect, is adduced as one of the most striking, if not the best specimen of beauty, that is to be found in the whole range of nature or art.

But the face of an idiot fails to reach this standard of pre-eminence. And next to this, is the simpering, senseless, conceited, self-applauding expression of a young lady, who has been flattered into the belief that she is a beauty, and who has thrown aside her books, and relinquished the labour of thought, for the toilet, and circles of fashion. My daughters, remember your minds are your estates. Education, like the diligent hand of cultivation, gives them permanent value, encloses, protects, and makes them fruitful. With this capital, well and diligently preserved from waste or decay, you may always be independent, and will soon surpass, in everything which can contribute to your peace and happiness, many who may now excel you in the contingent circumstances of fortune or personal attractions. In all circumstances, economy is a virtue; and no present elevation above want can secure us against the contingency of misfortune and poverty. Hence the habit of economy is always liable to be called into requisition, especially in a lady, whose means of repairing losses are more limited, and exposures to attendant evils greater than those of the other sex. Every young lady ought, therefore, to practise economy as a duty, if not from necessity, or under parental injunction.

He who limits his desires or annihilates a want, increases his riches more effectually than he who adds any amount of dollars and cents to his actual possessions. Our desires increase with our riches, but where want is extinguished wealth is virtually attained. The latter may be done in advance, under a well regulated and severe habit, but will hardly avail as a remedy for unsuccessful ambition. Modest pretensions can sustain unexpected promotion better than vaulting ambition can take the garb of humility and live contentedly on slender means. Habits of extravagance, once formed, present the strongest temptations to unlawful and sinful expedients to gratify those habits.

Our actual wants are really very limited and easily supplied. This may be readily shown by a reference to the peasantry of many other countries, and the slaves of our own. In the last example, their simple fare, while it evidently furnishes ample nutriment to fit them for ordinary labour, secures to them far better health than is enjoyed by their masters and others who live more luxuriously, and pay the price in physicians' bills, or disease and death.

Learn, then, to limit your expenses to your actual wants. This rule will always sufficiently swell the bills of a young lady at school, while the strict application of it will form a most valuable part of her education. Were I to seek for a practical lesson on this important subject, to direct your habits, I would refer to your recollections of your dear mother, whose personal expenses were ever as restricted as her personal appearance was always neat and appropriate. May you imitate her virtues in this as in every other department of duty.

## LETTER XXIX.

### PERMANENCY OF EARLY PRINCIPLES.

MY DEAR CHILDREN,—In the sports of children the seeds are sown whose fruits we reap in manhood. Every action is a starting point, that gives to the mind a direction, which may never be interrupted until eternity shall close in upon time, and its retributions shall be unalterably awarded. All, therefore, which is unworthy of manhood, is dangerous in youth, and the more dangerous because everything pertaining to character is then in a forming state.

Let these thoughts influence you in all your intercourse with your companions. There are no principles, that will ever belong to your intercourse with society which do not, with some modifications, belong to the social intercourse of youth at school. The affections you cherish, or the passions you indulge, will have a powerful influence to form your character to gentleness and truth, or to falsehood and crime. And where, more than in the intercourse of youth in a course of education, are exciting causes furnished to awaken the natural sensibilities of the heart? Here, then, "in the beginning of our way," sentinels should be posted, who may be always awake, lest a single misstep should change the whole direction of our being. We are here placed as at a central point. A thousand diverging lines lead to wide extremes, which grow wider still as we advance. A breath may, at the starting point, change our direction for eternity. But when settled and advanced in our course, a serious error may be more easily retrieved, and its consequences averted.

Think not, therefore, that because you are young, the terms, on which you live with your companions, are of little consequence; that you may indulge in fretfulness or ill humour, that you may cherish a pride of superiority, vain ambition, jealousy, envy, crimination, or revenge, and not have their spirit incorporated with your character. Cherish these feelings now, and they will establish a dominion over you, which your more deliberate decisions and self-reproach will not enable you successfully to war against in riper years.

Awakened attention to study is very apt to degenerate into unholy ambition. The effort, which is excited by the mere desire to surpass a rival, will be always attended with numerous and deep sources of irritation and pain, for the miseries of which, no success can compensate. The only remedy or preventive to such evils is the habit of prosecuting study, as every other employment, under a sense of duty. This may be a permanent principle, equable and efficient in its action, while ambition finds its impulse to exertion only in the presence of a rival, and is gratified only by his inferiority or downfall. It is not easy to determine, which is most fatal to true peace of mind, the exultation of triumph, or the chagrin of defeat. Both are blasting to every pious and holy affection of the soul.

So far as intellectual capacity is considered, a mediocrity of talent with good health, is the greatest blessing. With these endowments of nature, literary eminence is the sure result of studious habits. Genius, like personal beauty, is almost certainly a calamity. It excites admiration, and elicits applause. This soon begets in the mind a vain self-conceit of superiority. The mind, accustomed to praise, soon comes to a vitiated desire for it, which nothing else can satisfy. Like the sensual appetites, every indulgence blunts the sensibility, and makes it necessary to increase the dose. Often, too, the inspirations of genius are relied on instead of laborious study. While, therefore, more applause is constantly demanded, the excellence, which commands it, is diminished in the mind given to indolence and inflated by flattery; and the diligent student of ordinary genius soon surpasses the prodigy, whose youth is spent in self-admiration, and in listening to the indiscreet and often silly praises of thoughtless friends.

The mind, which gains its maturity only with manhood, is strengthened and rectified by an experienced acquaintance with real life, and learns, before they are felt, to estimate the rewards of praise according to their true value. The envy which may be awakened in the contemporaries of our early years, and which always embitters precocious honours, is dead or toothless before the title to those honours has been established by the service and trial of age, or when the subject of them stands almost alone among the survivors of his own generation. Although this view may present to your young minds a cheerless prospect in the distinctions of life, age and experience pronounce it the only prospect which can be cherished with truth. It is a most rich reward to an anxious and devoted parent, to see his children excel in their studies and labours. But I would much rather see you fail of the first honours in all that pertains to the distinctions of this life, than to see you subjected to the attendant temptations. Petrarch, an Italian of the fourteenth century, was crowned early in life with the poetic laurel. In future years, he wrote in view of the event thus: "These laurels, which encircled my head were too green. Had I been of riper age and understanding, I should not have sought them. Old men love only what is useful. Young men run after appearances without regard to their end. This crown rendered me neither more wise nor eloquent. It only served to raise envy, and deprive me of the repose I enjoyed. From that time, tongues and pens were sharpened against me; my friends became my enemies, and I suffered the just effects of my confidence and presumption."

The only value of eminence and success lies in the superior service, which we are thereby enabled to render to the great cause of truth and righteousness. The good that he does is itself the reward of the good man, whether his name is known and recognized in connection with the deed or not. The feeling, which finds its gratification only in the advancement of personal fame, is unholy, and is destined to the final disappointment, which, under the divine government, infallibly awaits and will arrest the unhallowed spirit of selfish ambition. May you learn to award liberally your approbation to the service of others, and to esteem your own acquirements, pretensions, and merits, with that modest reserve, which will always leave it to others to say to you, "Come up higher."

I believe you will not mistake me in these remarks. It is my desire that you should acquit yourselves well, and it is proper that you should be stimulated by a desire to please your parent and merit the approbation of all the good. But a simple desire for applause is a very foolish and a very dangerous one. The person who cherishes it deeply, will soon find himself seeking it by unworthy means. It is the fruitful source of envy towards others, vain pride in one's own attainments, a foolish egotism, and many other hurtful and disgraceful feelings.

Do you ask, from what motive you should strive to excel? Go to the Bible for the answer. Go to the death-bed—go to the grave—go to the rewards of eternity. There find the answer. Jehovah says, "Them that honour me, I will honour; and they that despise me shall be lightly esteemed." Find all your incentives to virtuous action in your relations to God and to eternity. Then, your aims will be high and ennobling. God will approve them, and return your efforts upon you with blessing. Then, if others excel, even if they are your rivals, you will not suffer your bosoms to burn with envy towards them. You will feel a pleasure at their prosperity, although your highest aims for yourselves may not be attained. If your efforts enable you to excel, you will not be puffed up with vanity at your superiority, but will be thankful to God for your success. Modest and condescending, you will not be led to think or speak often of yourselves in those comparisons, which make others appear to disadvantage, and which show a vain conceit of your own abilities and acquirements. This is the most disgusting egotism, and is the stamp of a little mind. It always forfeits to its possessor the little merit he may have in the esteem of others, and subjects him to ridicule or contempt.

Let the truth be deeply impressed on your minds that how much soever you may attain of knowledge, you can know but little compared with what remains to be known, or when compared with the great Author of mind and knowledge. Consider also, that all human learning is very much limited to objects, which are themselves transient and perishing. Consider that the only knowledge finally profitable is the "knowledge of the only true God, and Jesus Christ, whom he has sent." It is characteristic of this knowledge to teach its possessors humility, and to make them the more modest in their pretensions the higher they advance. May this be your crowning virtue and true understanding.

## LETTER XXX.

### SIMPLICITY OF CHARACTER.

My dear Children,—Simplicity of character, as opposed to artifice and dissimulation, is essential to our own deliberate self-approval, or the respect of others. We are fitted, by the great Author of our being, to act in a particular sphere, and are adapted to the regular and efficient discharge of duty there. Each has his peculiar characteristics, which he must learn, and so direct, that he may fulfil the duties they involve, and act well his part. In the just administration of God, we are required to give and do according to what we have and are. To know ourselves, and to act in the sphere assigned us by divine providence, is to do our duty and find its rewards.

Opposed to this simple purpose and pursuit is a deep laid disposition in every heart to play the hypocrite, to appear to be what we are not. It is developed in the earliest actions of childhood, and the reflecting mind has to combat its vigorous growth and struggles in riper years. Those who are insensible of its presence, who have never met in the war of self-conquest, are under its dominion still, unperceived only because the mind's subjection is complete.

Avoid the employment of artifice to make yourselves appear to others what you are not. This rule, which applies to those silly and wicked devices used by many to improve their form and person, it is my particular purpose, now, to apply to graver matters. Some attempt to appear more talented than nature has formed them, or more learned than their industry has made them. This affectation leads not only to folly but to sin. Often, a mind thus cultivated will be led to literary plagiarism to cover its ignorance or flatter its pride. Here is the sin of theft. The person who appropriates the literary labours of another as his own is a thief, as much as if he stole his neighbour's grain, or any other product of his labour. Then he is guilty of falsehood, by assuming publicly to have done what he never did. Not the least evil, however, is the self-deception and vanity which is thus cherished. The person who attempts to deceive others must first deceive himself. He must shut his eyes against a consideration of his own baseness, and first persuade himself that he is what he is not, an honest man. As he will not permit himself to suspect his own veracity, he will not allow others to impeach it, and will become testy in precise proportion to his default. As he affects to be learned, nothing will mortify his pride so much as to see his claims underrated. As he affects to respect himself, he will be deeply wounded by any want of respect towards him on the part of others. This, in the literary world, is an artificial man. Such may be found in every department, and of both sexes.

Whatever we hide of our deformities, or magnify of our actual attainments, will subtract double from our real merits when the deception is detected. You never extend your confidence to one who has once deceived you. You cannot do it. You may try, but it is impossible. On the other hand, honesty necessarily inspires confidence. You cannot withhold it. There may be few qualities to command admiration, or suited for various and difficult service—but an honest man commands confidence. Nature asserts his right in every heart, and he cannot be robbed of it until you misrepresent him.

Artifice and dissimulation are destined to final exposure and disgrace. Not to refer to that day when every action, every idle word, and every secret thought shall come into final judgment, the retribution of these shallow vices is usually awarded and suffered in this life. The precise and statue-like rouge, which gives its colour to a wrinkled cheek, is detected by its silence. It does not come and go like the blushes of nature, following and answering to the emotions of a living soul. The halting step of age betrays the antiquary who would take refuge under a dress and fashions that belong to a later century. And the ignoramus in literature, who has shone in borrowed wit, is unmasked the moment his fictitious reputation calls him to a service where there are no spoils furnished to his hand. But you cannot disgrace an honest man. He brightens with every disclosure. To dishonour, you must misrepresent him, and this cannot avail to his permanent disgrace. Call him ignorant;—he speaks, and demolishes your argument. And, true to the sentiment of the poet, we invariably prove that "beauty when unadorned, is adorned the most."

Artifice and dissimulation properly involve, to some extent, the character and guilt of falseness, because they present us in a false aspect, different from what we really are. The consequences are sometimes serious and important, and render the guilt of the crime enormous. Yet it is to be considered that true ingenuousness does not always require us to declare ourselves on every subject. We are often excited to strong emotions, which it may be our duty to suppress. Sometimes their suppression is necessary to the formation of a deliberate judgment; sometimes, that we may not throw ourselves into the power of our enemy; sometimes to the maintenance of a suitable influ ence over a friend. "Even the truth may not be spoken at all times." Not that we may tell a a falsehood in place of it, but real ingenuousness sometimes is consistent with silence. I have now in my mind the case of a gentleman who reported the personal remarks of one friend to another. It led to the evils of a duel. The reporter was greatly and justly blamed. It is not necessary that all which is true should be repeated at all times, and on common occasions. The most serious and disturbing evils often arise from that kind of frankness which will hold nothing but in common with a mixed and ever changing public.

## LETTER XXXI.

### PRUDENCE.

My dear Children,—Let *Prudence* be known in your vocabulary. Place it in the catalogue of your virtues, at the head of a chapter in your moral lessons. It is opposed to hasty and rash decision in enterprise, to obstinacy in pursuit, and to a reckless disregard of consequences.

"The only secret I have found," said Petrarch, "to prevent the evils of life, is to do nothing without having examined, beforehand, in what we are going to embark. In most things we undertake, the beginnings are agreeable. They seduce us. But we should think of the end. They are paths strewed with flowers. Where these paths lead to is the most important question."

Never are these sentiments more appropriate or more important than in application to the early period of life, when we are commencing in everything, and when our first choice is to give direction to a whole life, to an eternal life. Never will they come to your minds as appropriate instruction to make you wise so much as at the present moment, when you are young, and the paths of active life are yet untrodden.

Prudence teaches us to examine deliberately and well every enterprise, to which we are invited. She calls us into the field of thoughtfulness, of retirement, of meditation. She takes us away from the peculiarities, with which the subject may be attended, the false glosses and false forms, in which it may be presented in connection with the misrepresentations of interest or the recommendations of a public opinion, perhaps capriciously formed and capriciously changing. She invites us to think for ourselves, and form an independent judgment. She inquires how the highest law, the law of God, applies to the subject. She sets us down to the study of the Bible, and will allow us to make no important decision on any subject without asking counsel of God, and seeking at a throne of grace for that "wisdom which is from above, which is first pure, then peaceable, gentle, easy to be entreated, full of mercy and good fruits, without partiality and without hypocrisy."

Prudence will also lead us to review our decisions. If it teaches to guard against a ready admission of seeming difficulties in the prosecution of an object deliberately undertaken, it is, on the other hand, equally opposed to that inveterate obstinacy, which will admit no light that did not come at first. This is, as if we should refuse to consider, by the broad light of day, the dangers which were disregarded, because unseen, when we commenced our journey at midnight. Such adventurous spirits may be carried successfully through, but they will be very likely to be dashed over fatal precipices. Never to modify or even change our action in obedience to circumstances, is as wide from the dictates of true wisdom as to abandon ourselves to the changing advice and caprice of all we meet. A prudent man will often review his opinions. Sometimes the wisest prove themselves to have commenced in error. Their wisdom, then, shows itself in change of opinion, and of action. "To err is human"—to correct an error is the part of wisdom—"to forgive divine."

Prudence will lead us to a constant regard to consequences. The important truth has been often much perverted—"that duty belongs to us, consequences to God." Tell me what duty is, and I adopt the maxim—no matter what comes, self-indulgence or the stake, a crown or the cross. But our duty is often decided by the consequences of what we do, and therefore in most questions of duty, consequences are to be regarded, and to have their influence. If I am required to deny my Lord, my duty is plain, and I discharge it regardless of consequences, though it kindle upon me the fires of persecution, though it bind me to the stake, and consign me to death, and involve my murderers in damning guilt—"Duty belongs to me, consequences to God."

But suppose the question of duty relates to the reformation of my neighbour, and after I have faithfully reproved him, he remains impenitent and grows worse, and all my attempts to reform him, excite his passions, awaken and embitter old enmities, and involve his innocent family in greater evils—must I proceed? I say, not without regard to consequences. These consequences belong to me, and are a part of the grounds on which I am to decide my duty. True, I read in the great book of law—"Thou shalt in any wise rebuke thy neighbour, and not suffer sin upon him." But I have rebuked him; and I also read—"Cast not your pearls before swine, lest they trample them under their feet, and turn again and rend you." That is, have a suitable regard to consequences. Again I find divine counsel teaches us to be "wise as serpents, and harmless as doves." That is, act with caution as well as decision—*be prudent.*

When, therefore, I have discharged one part of my duty, by administering wholesome reproof to my neighbour, and by an attempt unsuccessfully made, to reclaim him, my next duty under the circumstances of the case, may be, to let him alone. So God sometimes does with sinners. But what he does in their final abandonment, it may be my duty to do in an untiring attempt to reform them. I may have become peculiarly obnoxious to my neighbour, either by my indiscretion or faithfulness. A spirit of jealousy may have taken possession of his bosom, so that he attributes, right or wrong, everything I do to a bad motive, to personal resentment, and hence my reproofs can do him no good, are even worse than useless. Perhaps there dwells by him, or in his own house, one to whom the duty to instruct and reprove him can with safety be committed, and to whom under the circumstances, it belongs. It may then be my duty to desist from doing the very thing, which before, it was my duty to do—and all this in regard to consequences. While, therefore, I would have you to be bold, and uncompromising in duty, I would have you prudently attentive to the circumstances, under which you act, and to the consequences, which will result from your action. Sometimes the most effectual reproof we can give to a captious sinner is to show him the difference between his life and ours, and to show our abhorrence of his sin by a refusal to participate in it. Sometimes even reproof of sin is made to appear unkind and bitter by the peculiar manner in which it is expressed, and the form in which it is repeated. Seek always to administer reproof so that the subject of it may find no ground to suspect it proceeds from personal un kindness or ill will.

Then you will not lose the respect of him whom you seek to reform, though you may fail to reclaim him.

That prudence which is so necessary in deciding our conduct toward others, in all our great efforts of benevolence, should also give character to all our conversation, and chasten all our intercourse with society. The maxims, which should regulate the entire deportment of a lady, especially a young lady, are those which the scriptures teach, where your sex is raised from a condition of mere subjection, and restored at once to the blessings of liberty and law. "Abstain from all appearance of evil," is a practical rule of universal application, and will ever present those who apply it, to the concurrent approbation and love of all. It will make you scrupulously attentive to all the decencies of life, and all the forms of society, so far as they involve proprieties, or are unattended with sin or temptation. It will adorn you with a "meek and quiet spirit,"—keep you at home—make you attentive to your own business—not "busy-bodies," nor "backbiters"—and in every relation you sustain, or may be called to sustain in life, the precious gospel, if you imbibe its spirit and follow its rules, will make you blessed and a blessing to others.

In your intercourse with mixed society, you will have occasion to cultivate that entire frame of mind and deportment, which are expressed by the term *prudence.* An imprudent lady can never be respected. Her influence is bad, and although the extent of her offence may be in the "appearance of evil," she will soon be taught by her reception in society that she has "trifled with a serious thing."

Nothing but a habit of reflection and forecast can throw around your character and happiness the best safeguards. I repeat then, avoid rash decisions; review them often; and consider well the consequences of what you do. It is indeed true, that "in most things we undertake, the beginnings are agreeable." They have, at least, the charm of novelty. "Where these paths lead to is the most important question."

I should be glad to furnish you with a striking illustration of what I mean by the trait of character so important in all, so vitally important in a female, and which I have now attempted to commend to your special consideration. Perhaps I cannot do it better than by stating a fact, which lately came under my own observation. A young lady of my acquaintance was addressed by a gentleman, then almost an entire stranger to her, but who was thought by all who knew him well deserving her hand. A mutual friend to them both said to him, You must not expect from her a hasty answer, for she is a prudent young lady. And so it proved. She considered the matter well, and was thereby enabled, I doubt not, to decide wisely.

## LETTER XXXII.

### INDEPENDENCE OF CHARACTER.

MY DEAR CHILDREN,—Independence of character pertains to us in the relations we sustain to society. It is particularly worthy of your consideration, that you may be guarded from error in the cultivation of it, and form your habits on principles which I pray may give in you stability to a character wisely framed and divinely approved.

Strictly speaking, independence can be predicated of God only. All other beings are dependent on him for life at first, for its preservation, and all its blessings. No man is absolutely independent, even of his fellow men. If the slave is dependent on his master for counsel, direction, food, raiment, and protection, the master is also, in some sense, dependent on the slave for the physical force necessary to the production, with the divine blessing, of his temporal comforts and means of happiness. The rich man is dependent on the mechanic for many of the common conveniences of life; on the artist for his refined pleasures of taste; on the butcher for his meat; the confectioner or gardener for his luxuries; on his cooks, not only for his relishes and well provided varieties of food, but for his daily bread.

There is much affectation of an independence, which does not and cannot pertain to man. Can wealth secure it? Let the proud pretension be asserted by the man who thinks so, and it is in the power of his shoe-black or washer-woman to prove its falseness. His tailor or barber can render him ridiculous. He cannot attend a pleasure party without being dependent on some dozen persons of different trades and professions for a happy entertainment. He cannot go before the public happily and advantageously, independent of several persons necessary to provide for, and administer to him. Let him not say he is rich, and therefore independent. Let him but fail to conciliate his lackeys; let him assert his absolute independence, and incur the enmity of the meanest servant in his train, or the humblest man that administers to his pleasures, and he will easily see that it is entirely in the power of that man to make him miserable; that the labours of that man are necessary to his happiness. He is dependent, in some sense, on all who are dependent on him.

When the mutual relations of different classes are properly understood and felt, all will be led to respect or treat all others in their respective stations according to their proper claims, and the order of Providence will then be found to secure the happiness of the whole. No one may be despised on account of his station, if it be an honest calling. If it be not honest, the man himself is guilty who will encourage or patronize him in it.

A proper sense of our mutual dependence is necessary to that mutual respect, deference, or treatment which will secure the highest happiness even of the most privileged, and secure the best good of society in the preservation of that order which is "heaven's first law."

The necessary dependence of every man is not limited to those things for which, although necessary to him, the rich man pays an equivalent. Every one is liable to need favours, and often obliged to receive them, for which no payment can properly be made, because they are priceless. Friendship cannot be bought. Sympathy in affliction—can gold gain that? Yet who may not need it, when wealth, in its greatest extent, sinks to airy nothing? The hand that wipes the tear which betrays the agony of a wounded spirit is insulted, mocked by the sordid wretch who should offer to wipe off his obligation by purchase money. There is something more—far more valuable than wealth. A friend is that treasure,—one who will prove faithful in adversity. There are acquisitions which are sometimes seen to elevate the menial far above his lord—it is a just sense of what is due to himself and to all others, and a faithful discharge, on his part, of those offices which belong to him, while he is treated, in return, with contumely and contempt. I would much rather be such a menial than such a master. In the wise retributions of the moral government we live in, the scales will be turned. That princely soul shall be exalted, though now a menial; and that mean spirit will be humbled, though now a prince.

Never scorn to receive a favour, nor be reluctant to confer one. There is no disgrace in the one, nor merit in the other. In giving, if we are able to do it, we are the almoners of divine bounty, and but imitate our great Master. In receiving, we but incur new obligations to the Giver of every good gift, of which our benefactor is made the privileged instrument. It is therefore declared to be "more blessed to give than to receive"—and hence the giver is really under the greatest obligations. The proper feelings which belong to the benefactor and the beneficiary are often mistaken, and those duties which are due only to God, are claimed by his agent in a work of charity, where he has the greater privilege of the two.

Let it not be contended, however, that the immediate benefactor has no special claims to gratitude and love. He appears in God's stead as God's agent, and while the blessings he brings, evidence a present God, and draw forth our gratitude to the great Author, man appears an humble imitator of the great Benefactor, when he scatters blessings with a liberal hand. • We love him for his likeness to his Master, and in contrast with the miser. We are made alive to his worth by the personal evidences we have felt of his benevolence. We, therefore, love and are grateful to our benefactor.

What then, it may be asked, is personal independence, and how far should it be sought? When applied to any other being than God, it is a relative term. All are dependent. Some are only less dependent than others.

We should always seek to be as little dependent as possible on others for everything necessary to our life and comfort. That is, we should provide for our own wants. At the same time we ought never to feel above the acceptance of a favour. We should be as willing to incur as we are ready to impose obligations. These mutual offices, when restricted to our real wants, serve to bind more closely the ties of friendship and mutual confidence; and hence the warmest friendships are usually found among the poor or middle classes, where these forms are most often reciprocated.

True independence is removed from contempt of others on one hand, and servile compliances on the other. It will never suffer the pride of superiority to despise or impose on the poor, nor a sense of obligation for a favour to lead us to a mean compliance. The moment the benefactor requires or asks a favour to be returned by a mean device, or a wrong act, he has more than cancelled the obligation,—he is himself the debtor; and the beneficiary, if he possess the true spirit of independence, will assert and maintain his own superiority.

A proper and commendable spirit of independence is necessary to divest us of the influence of men and circumstances, in forming our opinions. Here the merits of the subject alone should finally influence us. The decision of one in whom we have confidence may serve to incline us to his opinion or confirm us in our own, but should never be adopted as ours, simply because it is his. This remark applies, with particular propriety, to religious subjects. Here, the best qualification for a judge is singleness of heart and purpose. Mere learning and talents bring but little aid. The pride they cherish often obscures the mental vision, and embarrasses the judgment. The principal bar to a right decision on moral subjects is found in the state of the affections. When they are right, divine truth and duty are plain even to "the way-faring man." In all other cases they are hidden, even from the "wise and prudent."

We may be said to be independent so far as we can rely on our own resources for our special exigencies as well as for the supply of ordinary wants. This kind of independence is diligently to be sought. Without it to some extent there can be no fixed character, and our happiness will be placed very much at the disposal of others. How easily we learn to despise the person who cannot give an opinion on any subject until he has heard the opinions of others! Our respect and deference are reserved to the man who gives his own opinion with the reason of it. We can ask a favour with confidence and self-respect where it is a reciprocation of good offices, or of rare occurrence; but the man who goes frequently to his neighbour for that which his own industry ought to provide, will soon make his request in a servile manner, self-condemned, and under a wearisome sense of his own degradation.

In cherishing a spirit of independence, which I have earnestly recommended to you, some have degenerated into a disregard of the proprieties of life, and to a contempt of law. We can never be so independent of others as not to be seriously affected by public opinion, whose frown can be sustained only by a well founded self-approba-

tion, an approving conscience. Then only are we independent of the caprice of public opinion, when we are deliberately sustained by our own approbation. This is the only state of mind, which can lead us to that elevated course of action, which will be effective, and secure the eventual approbation of the public mind, sometimes slow in its action, but finally just in its awards.

We never can be, and ought never to desire to be, independent of law, whether the law of God or of man. The laws of God are always good, and are ever competent to correct our own erring judgment on every subject. Human laws, made for a common weal, are to be regarded so long as they are in force, and to be repealed, not by violence, but by legal enactments. It is often better to submit to a bad law than to resort to the last law of nature—rebellion. A public opinion which we may deem to be erroneous, may sometimes modify our conduct, where no principle is involved, and where we cannot control that public opinion.

Beyond this let nothing force you to go. Here the law of God enforces its rule, and duty is distinct. The highest obligation lies where religious duty marks your path. Never do wrong. Let no personal obligation be felt for a single moment in conflict with a sense of moral duty. No person living can ever confer upon you a favour, which can give any claim to your service, at the expense of your moral principle. He, who would ask it, forfeits everything, which his benefaction might otherwise claim.

## LETTER XXXIII.

### FEMALE EDUCATION.

MY DEAR CHILDREN,—Considered in our social relations, female influence is so paramount in its action, and so important in its results on every lasting interest of society, that no system of female education or duty can be suitably prescribed without a constant regard to that influence.

We are so constituted by nature, the very structure of our being is such, that the destiny of the race is instrumentally at the disposal of the weaker sex. This has been verified from the history of Eden to the present time. Society ever has been, and now is, and always will be, just what female character makes it, or permits it to be. Many philosophical causes might be adduced to show how this influence exists, but the fact is all I wish to advert to, in order to bring that fact into connection with the subject of female education.

The place which woman occupies, and the influence she exerts, must be considered before we can determine what her education should be, or what her proper duties are. She stands properly at the head of the race, and starts every new generation in their course. Her tempers, sentiments, and habits, are the first which come under the cognizance of infancy or childhood. They are, indeed, interwoven with our earliest actions, while those actions are almost involuntary or imitative. The sons and daughters receive their mother's advice as the highest law. The husband regards her heart as the hallowed depository of all that is pure, and society receives its laws from her sense of propriety or of right. Every daughter and son, every confiding husband, and every man can testify to the controlling influence of the mother, the wife, the sister, the female in society, placed as its presiding ornament, and dictating its common laws.

Here, then, in the place she is to occupy, and in the influence she is to exert, we are to look for the true reasons which should direct the education of females, and determine what it should be.

First, she is to occupy the place, and exert the influence of a mother. I speak now of the race. Here, under divine appointment, she applies the plastic hand to a moral and intellectual substance, at its starting point for eternity. None will deny that the children of every family take their character principally from the mother of that family. Through life, they yield fruit according to the seed sown, the character imprinted in the nursery and in the parlour. Through eternity they retain this character. What kind of education can qualify her to discharge the arduous and responsible duties of such a situation? If the physical nature of that child is disordered, the learned and skilful physician is called in to prescribe. To administer spiritual instruction and relief, requires the learning of a divine; and the masters in intellectual philosophy alone are competent to its intellectual training. Here we see what sort of education that mother needs. She must know, and know intimately, the physical, intellectual, and moral nature of the being she educates, and be able to apply the principles of the true philosophy in the training of it.

The influence of a mother's counsel and a mother's care might be referred to, if additional support were needed to affirm this position. The mother's hand laid upon the feverish temple, that kind hand is for ever remembered. That touch is felt as if there were an abiding impression made by it, perhaps through life. The moral instruction she then whispered in the ear remains bright and impressive in memory's store-house. The looks of love or gentle reproof, of approbation or censure, exist like durable forms in the mind. The mother is ever before the mind; and when the pride of intellect has transported the man in maturity beyond the influence of even sound argument and rational conviction, he remembers the lessons of that mother and feels their truth. By a law of his nature, he is held by that mother's influence, and whenever he feels it, he becomes docile. I may here illustrate my remark by a reference to the testimony of the celebrated, witty, eccentric, and eminent John Randolph. Through a life uncommonly various in public incident and honours, he said to a friend, "I should have been an infidel, had it not been for the influence exerted on me by my mother, as she taught me to kneel at her side, and fold my little hands, and say, 'Our Father who art in Heaven,'" &c.

Similar results will be found, if we consider the power of female influence in all the other relations of life, as a wife, a daughter, a sister, or a friend. She always exerts a great, often a controlling influence.

Look into families. Who regulates the terms of social intercourse? Who gives character to the conversation, and who prescribes laws there? It is the mother, daughter, sister, the female members of the family. The husband, father, brother, the young men of every community, are influenced in every department of labour and of duty by a constant reference to the opinions, the approbation of those whom they may meet in the hallowed society of home. Here is the centre of influence.

The man is brutal, who can see unmoved a tear on the cheek of an affectionate wife; who can willingly excite a blush for a father's wrong on a daughter's face, or wound a sister's confiding feelings, or trifle with a lady's frown. Gentlemen are accustomed to speak and act as they think will meet the approbation of female society. This fact shows at once the importance that the sentiments of females should be such as to form a correct standard of public opinion, and their conversation embrace a range of subjects worthy of the attention of men, of immortal men; subjects suited to the great duties of life, the interests of an eternal life.

The place, then, which the female occupies in society, and the influence she exerts, require the most complete moral and intellectual education to prepare her for her duties. She may not only "learn to read, and write, and cipher," but she ought to have her mind and character formed by whatever can adorn or give strength to the intellect. And why should she not? She has a whole life to live—why not spend it rationally? She must always be doing something. The mind must think. Why may she not as well be wise as frivolous? Why may she not as well be devoted to literature as to fashion? Why may not the conversation of mixed companies, which occupies so large a share of our time and attention, be rational, literary, and improving, instead of being, as it too often is, vain, unprofitable, and dissipating?

Every view we can take of the bearing of female influence on the character and destiny of our race, enforces the importance that female education should be of the most substantial kind. Except as a means of reaching after higher attainments, I think but little of a young lady's ability to paint a rose or mould a wax flower. I would rather see you able to analyze the flower itself, plucked in its season, fragrant with its native sweets, glowing with its native, inimitable colours, and enamel. I prize at a low rate the graces, which consist in exact and measured movements, performed in the mazy dance. I would have you cultivate a sound understanding, and quick sense of propriety in all your intercourse with society, in all your intercourse with yourselves. The character which will be thus formed under the influence of a meek and quiet spirit, will recommend you to approbation, when every design of art will fail.

I would not have a lady inattentive to her person, much less neglectful of the ordinary forms of social intercourse. But I give it to you as the deliberate result of my observation on society, that true grace of personal manner, so far as that is a subject of education, depends far more on a correct sense of propriety, and on intellectual education, than on any physical training of the dancing-master, or rules of art. A ride on horseback, or a botanical ramble, or a walk in the fresh air of the early morning, or even the necessary effort to put your own room in order before you leave it, furnish a more uniform and safer exercise, uniting the "*utile cum dulci*," the pleasant and profitable, than all the physical discipline which can result from mere pleasure or constraint. I would rather see you able to cook well a penny loaf, or lead a charity enterprise, than to cut the "pigeon wing" in "measured motion," or to dance a cotillion.

A reference to the condition of females in society, is necessary to justify the manner in which I have directed your education. My object has been, here, to lead your minds to consider intelligently the subject of female education in its general bearing, that you may be prepared to apply principles to practical use, and be led to contribute your influence to the adoption of just notions of it. Whatever may contribute to elevate the standard of female education, and to promote a proper influence, adds weight to a lever of tremendous power and lengthens its shaft.

## LETTER XXXIV.

### EARLY EDUCATION.

My dear Children,—The reason why there are so many in maturity of years who can neither read with propriety, nor spell correctly, is, that this part of their education has been neglected until habits of inattention were confirmed, and the spelling-book was beneath their ambition. This part of elementary education being neglected, correctness will hardly be attained in anything else.

Accuracy and facility in reading and spelling were among your earliest attainments. At the age of four years, this part of your education was completed. And what was done for you, every mother may do for every child. It is best and easiest done at this early age. Arithmetical accuracy you acquired almost as early. Elementary arithmetic, on which are based all the higher and most abstruse calculations, belongs to the studies of childhood, and may, to some extent, be incorporated with the amusements of the nursery. Children may as well amuse themselves with the multiplication table, and in adding, subtracting, or dividing, as with wax toys and marbles, and much better than with fairy stories and fiction. It is just as easy to give their books the charm of novelty and play-things, as to associate with these means of instruction the idea of pains and penalties. When children begin to think and reason, their taste is in a forming state, and it receives direction according to the objects presented to their attention. They will count their fingers with just as much pleasure as they roll a marble, and learn a psalm of David, or a ditty, with equal facility. It belongs to the mother and those connected with the nursery to give direction to their minds, always active and acquisitive of whatever subjects are furnished to them. There is thought. It cannot be destroyed. But it may, to a great extent, be controlled, directed, and modified. And never so easily as at that point where its action commences, and its first direction is taken. If profitable and pious thoughts are not the most easily introduced, it is nevertheless practicable to interest the mind in objects that are useful, and, to a great extent, combine amusement with useful labour.

Elementary geography and grammar also belong to the studies of an early age. If their higher principles and collateral branches require a mature understanding, yet these studies may be commenced almost as early as children begin to talk and think. Example, and use, and a few definitions early made familiar, will ensure to children a grammatical correctness, which philosophers, having been neglected in early life, have not been able afterwards to attain. A geographical map is a picture with which a child may become interested while he is instructed, and his habits of attention confirmed.

With such a preparation in a judicious elementary education, a young lady is prepared to enter profitably the boarding-school. If not thus prepared, she must spend at least one year after she enters, in these preparatory studies, or always feel embarrassed for want of them.

Mental discipline is the first object to which all education should be directed in the management of children, and in the entire instruction of youth. Hence the importance that the mothers first, and all teachers who may come after her, should be well versed in the philosophy of the mind. The mental constitution is the same. Education, therefore, in every stage, is based on the same principles. How perfectly preposterous then to separate from these principles the education of females, who exert the greatest influence on the whole character of our race! How unnatural to subtract the severer studies from female education, while they are prescribed to the other sex! If the exact sciences and philosophy are to be confined to one of the sexes, I do not hesitate to say, these studies should be excluded from the College, and given to the education of our daughters. And for the simple reason that they need them more to form their characters, and prepare them for their duties.

The seat of power should be the source of a salutary and saving influence. This power we readily yield to our wives and daughters, and then cast into that fountain noxious drugs instead of a cleansing and wholesome influence. We award to them the control of vital interests, yet educate them rather to trifle than to preside over our public and private morals. I will not contribute to this grand mistake. I will neither flatter in you feelings which are capable of being inflated with pride, nor trifle with responsibilities, which must rest upon you as educated and intelligent females. A just estimate of yourselves and your relations is necessary to prepare you for your duties and rewards.

## LETTER XXXV.

### ELEMENTARY STUDIES, HABITS OF STUDY.

My dear Children,—The elementary education of a female should always embrace a fair hand writing, facility in arithmetical calculations, book-keeping, and the common forms of business. If she may not be prepared to do business as a part of her appropriate duty, the importance of these qualifications is demonstrated in the frequency with which she is called by necessity to exercise them. These, added to an accurate knowledge of her native tongue and geography, all thoroughly learned, form a basis of education on which every lady may build and practise so as to render herself useful, respectable, and truly independent. I say these thoroughly learned—for there are many young ladies who have passed through the classes, even where they have been thoroughly taught, almost as ignorant as before.

There are several causes which will be found to be prolific, one or all of them, of this result. The most common, perhaps, is the great mistake of some young ladies in regard to the end they were made for, and the realities of future life. They are much indulged, and think they shall always be indulged. Under a parental sympathy they are protected, and never reflect that there are any to be met with, who will not feel it a privilege and duty to protect them. To provide for themselves, therefore, or depend on their own resources, is what they never learn, never practise. They spend their appointed time at school, eager to return to an indulgent home. It is no privilege to study, and, for a female, it is thought to be quite incongruous to study hard. Thus a habit of idleness is easily cherished. Time is wasted. A stolen glance at the text-book, or the aid of a more diligent classmate whispering in the ear what is uttered in parrot recitation, passes them, hesitating, blushing, and blundering, through their routine of tiresome study, until the quarter ends, a brother comes, pays the bills, and takes the young lady home with her education finished, but with no certain ideas, and with no serious conviction that life is anything to her but a summer's day, a "season's glitter." Many young ladies are never taught to consider, and therefore never learn, that the realities of life belong to them. To be waited on, flattered, and caressed, is all they have experienced, and, as this pleases them very well, it is all they care to expect. How sad the disappointment, when it comes! And come it must, if death do not interterpose to prevent.

I would have you provide for what may come. Be prepared for the worst, and then you will be prepared for all else, as the greater includes the less. I have endeavoured, therefore, to adapt your education to the place assigned you in providence, to consult utility in the plan, and thoroughness in the whole. Always feel that your present duties are part of the labours of life; that nothing can be slighted or carelessly done without affecting great and lasting interests. Be laborious, be thorough, be accurate, inquisitive, persevering.

Be laborious. Diligence is a duty imposed on all. Most persons find themselves finally forced to it. It is a contradiction of nature to affect perpetual leisure, and despise employment. She who attempts it, will soon become the slave of slaves.

Be thorough and accurate. What is well done is twice done. This is true, without a figure. What is not done well, needs soon to be done again. What is well done does not soon come to repairs. In study, this is especially true. The scholar of feeble effort and superficial habit is not certain that he knows anything. If called to the exercise of his learning, he blushes, stammers, hangs his head, guesses, is not certain, and as he never depends on himself, can never be depended on by others. But he who has once thoroughly acquired the principles of a science, is ready to apply those principles with confidence and success; goes fearlessly forward; is sensible he is acquainted with the ground, or can explore it. He is not, therefore, easily disconcerted. He speaks confidently and acts decidedly where the nature of the subject admits of certainty, and if it is doubtful in itself, he does not easily betray his ignorance by assuming a confident manner, or affecting what he does not understand.

Endeavour to know with certainty whatever you undertake to investigate, whatever you venture to act upon, especially whatever you profess to teach to others. How necessary this is in the most important matters! How necessary in personal religion, where a fatal mistake is final ruin; yet as we lay the foundation so shall we meet the storm! He that is unjust in the least will be unjust also in much. If we treat our ordinary duties loosely, we shall be likely to carry the same defective manner into the most serious, the most sacred, into our eternal interest.

Be inquisitive, not intermeddling. Never be ashamed to ask a question unless it be improper in itself, or your ignorance is the result of your idleness or neglect. Even then you ought to be more ashamed to remain in ignorance than to ask a question. Questions are the keys of knowledge. Those who use them most frequently will find the greatest treasures, and be able to appropriate them.

Be persevering. Never leave a subject until you understand it. Examine and continue your examinations on everything you fail to understand, and which deserves your effort. Never yield to difficulties merely because they are difficulties. These may be overcome, and if we are easily diverted by them we shall fail in everything, for what subject is entirely divested of them?

## LETTER XXXVI.

### COURSE OF STUDY—MENTAL DISCIPLINE.

My dear Children,—Among the best labour-saving expedients, whether in study or business, is a thorough habit of judicious classification. Reduce everything to system, whether you are engaged in study, in labour, or mere amusement. This habit once acquired, will enter into every department of life. It will regulate a young lady's toilet, as well as arrange the business of a Minister of State, and, in its measure, be as convenient and useful in the one as the other. Begin it early. Practise it in everything. It has been taught you in the nursery, and by maternal example. It constitutes a part of that mental discipline, to which I have already alluded, and which has been too much overlooked in female education. The attention of females in a course of education has been directed too much to mere accomplishment in what is superficial, light and pleasing. Hence vanity, trifling and useless ornament, have come of a taste thus formed. Hence the ancient imputation which has passed into a proverb, "*varium et mutabile semper femina.*"

Mental discipline is the thing—the great material in education. Acquisition is its end. That follows the education of the mind, as the effect the cause. Mental discipline, then, is education. It is the power to acquire knowledge, and convert the acquisition to the most productive effect. It is an unfailing capital, in itself a productive principle, which may be used at pleasure.

The education of a young lady is often made to consist of a few definitions or ideas, learned by rote, and floating in the mind without any form, arrangement, or symmetry of parts. In such a course, she could never have been interested, nor can she be profited by the results. What if she has a few ideas on botany, mineralogy, ethics, and astronomy, and the whole circle of liberal study and the arts. She cannot converse on either, nor convert her knowledge to any useful practical purpose. If, as a housewife, her bread has become sour in the rising, she will not know how to apply an antagonist principle to restore it; if her dress is soiled by carelessness, or accident, she will be unable to give the faded silk its lustre. The bread must be thrown away, and a new dress provided. Remember education is designed for practical purposes, and it consists of principles which are worthless unless in some way applicable to common life. In this application it will often enable the well taught housewife to save a joint which seemed almost unfit for the table, and sometimes to remodel an old dress, where prodigality or ignorance resorts to a new purchase.

The powers of the mind, like other powers, like the mechanical powers, if you please to take the comparison, must be used skilfully to produce their best effect. We must learn what they are, and how to direct them—then they may become effective. We may employ them extensively, and gather something worth preserving from every body and everything we meet. Judicious mental discipline forms an acquisitive mind, which, as it is always accumulating, must, at length, become learned. By the resolution of everything into its simple or elementary parts, it learns most easily its qualities, and comprehends the whole at the least possible expense of labour. Genius itself is but the power to "analyze and combine, amplify and animate." Thus, by a judicious education, if genius be not created, it is sometimes surpassed.

When it is considered how extensively the female part of the family is connected with the principal expenditures, how much they may aid in every system of retrenchment or saving, we may see how much better is learning than ignorance, and how much it affects all the great interests of the family through the wife and daughters. Some of the most elegantly neat and best dressed ladies of my acquaintance have limited the annual expense of their wardrobe to fifty dollars · and I have known others who appeared to less advantage with an expenditure of five hundred. The financial expense of families decides, in a great degree, the wealth of a nation. Female education, therefore, should be directed to this important consideration, and all ought to be taught how to calculate, to keep their own accounts, and estimate the value of a dollar. This can be secured only by a plan of education, which shall effect the due cultivation of all the intellectual powers, and subject them to a thorough discipline, which shall lead a female to the choice of the useful, and the rejection of the vain, useless, or immoral. How else can she be taught to feel the responsibility which lies connected with pecuniary expenditure, both as it regards the ability of her father or husband, and as it respects the calls of benevolence and charity? How else can she be expected to use money under a due sense of moral duty, or with honest regard to all other claims on the funds she appropriates? Moral education depends intimately on mental discipline. Without the latter, moral decisions are liable to be capricious and partial. As mental discipline gives stability to character, it effects, if not the moral constitution, the firmness and energy of moral action.

Instead, therefore, of passing a young lady

from the elementary to the ornamental branches of education, she should proceed to the severer studies in the exact sciences. Geometry and algebra should, by all means, form a part of a liberal education for a young lady. I have seen an almost entire change wrought in the mental habits of a young lady by the study of Euclid. This science cannot be prosecuted without bringing the reasoning and thinking powers to an active and well balanced labour. The lesson cannot be recited unless it is understood. There is no collusion. Nothing but study, close study, hard study can avail. Everything is distinctly marked. All is demonstration. It is known, or it is not known. The scholar is approved in her recitation, or shrinks into blushes and self-condemnation.

When the preparatory steps have been taken, algebra becomes an amusement. I do not mean to say it presents no difficulties, but its difficulties are not insuperable, and they furnish, in their successive subjugation, the constant pleasure of conquest. Like a traveller ascending a mountain, the diligent scholar in geometry and algebra goes from height to height, and from cliff to cliff, rewarded for every successive effort by a purer sky, a wider survey, and multiplying forms of beauty. At length he passes the regions of ordinary clouds, and rejoices in a sunshine unknown to the hum ble inhabitant of the vale beneath. If serenity of mind can be found short of moral causes, it must be the boon of the successful scholar, resting in triumph on the heights, or at the summit of the hill of science, self-conscious of his superiority, the reward of knowledge, enterprise, and persevering labour. Such is the geometrician at the end of his demonstration; the algebraist with his problem solved; the successful scholar in every step of his progress.

While I would include geometry and algebra in the ordinary course of female education, I do not think the higher branches of pure mathematics should be commonly attempted. But natural philosophy and astronomy should not be omitted. They embrace, we may say, the geometry of the known universe. This is the true field of devotion, and nowhere but at the cross can be found equal illustrations of the transcendent attributes of God. If you may not sit down to the *Principia* of Newton, nor attempt to solve the problems he left unsolved, you may yet demonstrate the theory of the universe, and without the power of prophecy calculate an eclipse, and foretell some of the most wonderful changes in nature. You may admire God in his works, above the reach of vulgar minds. You may rise to a new field of devotion, and find new motives of gratitude and love.

Intellectual and moral philosophy will come in of course, and, in my opinion, belong to a much earlier stage in education than is commonly assigned to them. We ought to know what can be known of the mind as early as we are capable of understanding it, and the elements of moral science belong to the first studies. Its higher principles should be taught *pari passu* with the ability to comprehend. Rhetoric and the higher principles of grammar, together with history, ancient and modern, I would refer to a later period. The natural sciences belong to common life and common education. I would have you good botanists, and not ignorant of chemistry and mineralogy. Geology should take enough of your attention to enable you to understand the structure of the earth and its general features. This is of practical importance, and almost necessary to an intelligent acquaintance with history and geography. This is a department where superficial study is impossible. Whatever you understand will be a valuable possession, although it may be of small amount. Like gold, it is good in its kind, and can be converted to a valuable purpose, although you may have but a small portion.

The study of language is important, both for practical utility, and also for its influence on mental discipline. While its grammatical structure is simple and easily comprehended, its philosophical principles are fitted to exercise the higher intellectual operations. Its principles are the same in every dialect; and once understood, they are of universal application. The Latin I consider necessary to a liberal female education, very useful, and by all means to be embraced in an extended course. It is called a dead language, and yet it is more universally known among the literati than any other. Besides its utility, the study of it constitutes a mental exercise of great value. If we except the Greek, it is the most complete in its structure, and the most varied in its adaptations to communicate thought, if not more copious in its resources, than any other language. If practicable, I desire also that you should read the Greek and Hebrew Scriptures; I would have you aim at this attainment, not so much for the valuable addition it would make to your stock of learning, as for the pleasure and profit of reading the Bible in its original languages.

Music is now considered a necessary part of a finished education for females. I think it should be so considered. First, vocal music, which is always the best, and the foundation of all other. Cultivate it, not merely, nor principally as an accomplishment, nor as an amusement, but as a science, and for its moral effect, as a means of praising God and awakening devotion. Learn to sing well if you can. Learn to play well, especially on the organ and piano. Praise God with the voice, and in the united harmony of every sound.

Drawing and painting I do not assign to the class of mere accomplishments. They are studies of real utility. Familiar practice in linear design, perspective, and landscape painting, promotes habits of attention and discrimination of great importance in practical life. She who draws with her pencil the outline of an edifice, will ever afterwards have her attention awakened to criticise the architectural proportions of other buildings. If she attempt a landscape, or pencil a rose, she will, in that effort, direct her attention with greater minuteness of discrimination to every flower she plucks, to every scene of nature. This is the great practical benefit of drawing and painting—not so much to furnish amusement, as to cultivate a taste and improve a faculty.

There are some other branches of female education, which I pass over as incidental. They may be omitted without material injury, and the cultivation of them should depend on circumstances of time, talent, genius, and facilities. Such is almost all, which is called "fancy work." I would not stifle a genius in an attempt to avoid them, nor force a taste. Let nature dictate.

## LETTER XXXVII.

### ON READING.

My dear Children,—Miscellaneous reading will occupy but little of your attention, while engaged in a course of study at school. Still you will find some time to read, and your selection of books is a matter of some importance, since it will strongly influence your taste, and style, and modes of thinking. Some remarks, then, on reading, may be of use to you. I shall limit these remarks rather to your present necessities than attempt to embrace a full course of reading, which may be deemed suitable at a future time. In what I now say, however, I shall strike the outline of an entire course, and if I should never return to the subject again, you may find in the advice of these letters the principles which should direct you in all your reading.

Place, then, at the head of your library, the *Bible.* Let it lie on your centre table, place a copy of it in your sleeping chamber, and in your closet. Let a place be found for it in your reticule. Travel with it. What was so beautifully and comprehensively said by Cicero of literary pursuits in general, may well be confined in strictness and truth to Biblical studies: "Other studies are suited neither to all times, ages, nor places. These improve youth, render old age pleasant, adorn prosperity, furnish a refuge and consolation in adversity, make home delightful, do not encumber us abroad, remain with us day and night, travel with us, and animate the solitude of the country."*

In Biblical studies I embrace not only the reading of the Bible in the manner I have already defined for devotional purposes, but the examination of its claims, both external and internal, to inspiration, its critical analysis, comparison, and interpretation. In fine, I include what is commonly embraced in Biblical literature and criticism. This branch of study belongs not only to the Theological Seminary and Biblical student, it is profitable for every one as far as means and leisure to pursue it are furnished. These collections are well worthy of the eulogium expressed by Cicero, on the studies of poetry and the arts.

---

* Cicero. Orat. pro A. Licinio Archia Poeta.

Nam ceteræ neque temporum sunt, neque ætatum omnium, neque locorum; hæc studia adolescentiam alunt, senectutem oblectant, secundas res ornant, adversis perfugium ac solatium præbent; delectant domi, nec impediunt foris; pernoctant nobiscum, peregrinantur, rusticantur.

If you seek for variety, elegance, or the sublime in composition, it is there. There is the most important and authentic history, and all that can charm in story and song. There is every variety of composition, from the simple language of childhood to the deepest pathos and the highest strains of eloquence, and the inspirations of poetry. There is matter for deep research, a mine of wealth, which the scholar, the historian, and critic, may never exhaust, and yet there is a soil rich with food for infant minds, and suited to every taste. The profane respect it; the enlightened infidel commends its morality; the scholar admires its learning; it instructs the humblest mind; all pay it homage. Read the Bible. Make it your manual, and if you aspire to investigate it in its original languages, you shall have my approbation and assistance. We recede from the fountain * as translations of the original are relied on.

Auxiliary to the Bible,† make use of the most approved commentaries without regard to sect or denomination, taking care always to deduce your own opinion from the text, with their help, and never go to them for your opinion.

Next to the Bible, and the helps necessary to a critical examination of it, let your reading em-

---

* Hebrœi bibunt fontes, Græci rivos, nos paludes.

† "Lege Biblia, relege Biblia, repete, iterum et saepe, Biblia."

brace religious biography, and the memoirs of pious men and women. Here you see examples of real life, and that kind of experience which can most effectually be converted by us to practical utility. We read the trials, labours, discouragements, and triumphs of the saints. Their diaries and records of personal experience are made under such circumstances, that we can place implicit confidence in them. They serve as lights and shades to direct our path, or warn us of dangers. Men, acting under the controlling influence of pride, ambition, or selfishness, cannot have our confidence, and their experience furnishes to us no safe and wholesome lesson. But here we are let into the inner temple, and read in the private diaries of good men their secret thoughts and inmost trials, which were never uttered to human ear. The psalms of David have something of this character, and are therefore peculiarly suited to aid in closet devotions and private meditations.

## LETTER XXXVIII.

### ON READING.

MY DEAR CHILDREN,—As this is a book-making age, many books of different characters will be thrown in your way. Let me give you some rules for trying their claims to your attentive reading. "Some books," says Lord Bacon, "are only to be tasted, others to be swallowed whole, others to be masticated and digested," and I will add, others should not be touched. Treat them as you do noxious plants. Some show the characteristics of the poisonous family in their bud and blossom. Their very foliage betrays them. Their leaves are not only bitter to the taste, they offend every sense. Others conceal their virus, and never betray it but in its fatal effects. It is grateful to the eye, taste and smell, but rankles in the blood, inflames the passions, subjugates the affections, kills the soul.

Sometimes the title page will indicate truly the character of the work. Like all other professions, however, this may be deceptive. The table of contents will generally give you a clue to a true estimate of what follows. The preface may furnish additional aid. After consulting these, endeavour to find in the general divisions, some distinct propositions, which are the author's starting points. Having proceeded thus far, you may often be possessed of the true merits of the work, and decide without farther waste of time, whether it should be studied, only cursorily perused, or wholly rejected.

Whenever you take up a book, before you proceed to read it, endeavour to know something of the author. All are human, and every production will be found to be influenced by human frailties. Does he call on you to receive facts? Even these facts may be stated with greater or less confidence, as his sympathies, or partialities, or prejudices, may dictate. Does he reason on those facts? His reasonings will be liable to a similar influence. Some of the best writings must be received with these abatements or cautions. For instance, among the best historians are reckoned Hume and Gibbon. But their bitter enmity to religion is often insidiously infused into the "History of England," and the "Decline and Fall of the Roman Empire." As the strongest prejudices generally prevail on religion and politics, you should seek especially to know the author's views on these subjects.

You will, of course, devote a portion of time to

reading during life. The rule, which I would prescribe for you, after what I have already said, is this: read what is most useful, and what will prepare you best for the end of life by exciting a diligent and conscientious discharge of its duties. You should not be ignorant of the different classes of composition, in the different departments of learning. But there are many books, and perhaps this includes the largest share, that are either directly pernicious, or otherwise unworthy of your attention. You cannot read all. Make, therefore, a judicious selection. Waste as little time as possible on those which are not positively good.

In regard to the comparative claims of different departments of reading, good sense, with a good education, is better than any written rules to direct. A well balanced education will enable any one to form her own decision, and I prefer to place you on your own judgment, rather than indulge you in a constant dependence by furnishing a detail which ought to exercise your own diligent investigation. It is necessary to a vigorous and healthy action of the mind, that it be left sometimes to its own independent choice. In the order of subjects, history will follow naturally after biography. Treatises on science, especially moral and intellectual, will be taken up in connection with the studies to which they respectively belong. Miscellaneous works must find their appropriate place amid the settled currents and established outlines of a systematic course. A few select periodicals should furnish you with a "bird's eye view" of the literature and passing news of the day. We have several little works well suited to female reading, while there are others professedly designed for them, which I would have you especially avoid.

I would not have you to become politicians, nor affect to volunteer grave opinions on political subjects. Yet I would not have you ignorant of passing political events, nor even of general politics, so far as your leisure may enable you to embrace the subject incidentally in your studies. A lady may appear amiable and modest in manifesting an interest in everything which affects the public weal, but always awkward and beyond her sex, when debating the principles of politics, or mingling in party feuds.

After what I have said, it would be superfluous for me to go into a laboured disquisition on novels, and the claims of that large class of reading to your attention. Give them the place they deserve. With the Bible at the head of your library, and eternity in prospect, and the duties of the present life pressing upon you, give to the reading of novels that portion of time and attention which your own good sense will dictate; and if this will not lead you to a wise decision, I am suro that decision is beyond the reach of any argument I can add. You are rational, moral, immortal, now concerned with the realities of life, soon to answer for the manner in which you have performed its sober duties. Let these weighty truths ever influence your decisions and give direction to your energies.

## LETTER XXXIX.

### ON READING.

My dear Children,—The library and reading of a young lady should be very select. Remember your books are your companions, your familiar, retired, confidential companions. Be careful, then, in the selection of them as you would in the choice of living associates. Take to your companionship none who are not worthy of your confidence. They will have their influence upon you. If you meet them in company, you may not be called upon to spurn them. That might appear like affectation. But I should be sorry to find you well acquainted with many authors, whose works are at this day often found in good company. I do not see why it is necessary, that, in order to be literary, we should be familiar with all authors of all kinds, any more than in order to know human nature, we should be familiar with the low and vicious. We may know what they are without taking them to our society; and that knowledge of their character should exclude them from familiarity. If I see certain characteristics in a female, I may understand her character without going to her house, which is "the way to hell." So, you may be sufficiently well acquainted with some authors by reading their title page, or at most, by learning their first proposition.

Life is short. There are good books enough to fill up all your time. Why, then, squander half of it on trifles? When you can no longer find good company, there will be time enough to parley with the bad—and then, if you are wise, you will live alone, rather than receive such into your society.

Among the books to be avoided, I place first and foremost Byron's Works. They cannot be read without mental pollution. It is impossible, constituted as we are, to read them, and escape from a train of associations most demoralizing and pernicious. After having embraced the tempter, we struggle in vain to extricate ourselves. He has insinuated himself imperceptibly into our bosoms, breathed upon the sanctuary of our devotions, and hung pictures upon the walls we can never obliterate nor remove. To the mind that has read Don Juan, there are the images naked in their deformity; and although they may be washed away at the gate of heaven, there is no controlling power in fallen man to relieve him from the spectre.

Care cannot be too diligently bestowed to chasten that prudery of a jealous temper, which is ever on the alert for causes of offence, and that prurient imagination which gives the worst construction to everything seen and heard. Where no offence is meant, we should be slow to take it, as a prompt resentment of designed insult is the only proper vindication which a lady can make of her own rights. There is much expressiveness in the sentiment of the apostle—"to the pure, all things are pure." This, however, cannot alter, and was not intended to alter, the nature of things. While we "think no evil," even unworthy allusions will pass unnoticed and innoxious; but there are some forms and some expressions which it would be the affectation of insensibility to disregard, as it would palpably confound the necessary distinctions between virtue and vice. This holds true of the works of Byron.

But Byron is brilliant, splendid, glowing with the inspirations of poetry. Yes, and that creates the illusion. Let his vulgar stories be told in doggerel, or plain prose English, and they would disgust. But Byron encircles them with brilliants, covers them with diamonds, dissolves the dose, and we take it and die!

I have read Don Juan, and therefore can advise you. I do advise you to avoid it as you would avoid a moral pestilence. It is no relief to say that all his works are not equally injurious, or that some are harmless, or even excellent. When I see an expurgated edition of Byron's works, worthy of a young lady's perusal, I will inform you. But I shall by no means recommend you to a house of bad character, because you may meet with some respectable people there. In the best society, you may encounter unworthy members, but there they are controlled. Here they exercise authority, and their influence is paramount. I say, therefore, "Avoid it; pass not by it: turn from it, and pass away."

In its moral influence, I regard this as decidedly the worst book in the English language. There is no composition of palpable vulgarity, but carries along with it its own materials to disgust. But this is an insidious poison. Constellations of wit, and brilliant coruscations of genius, breathed out and afflated by the inspirations of poetry, present a burning firmament of images, to attract and bewilder. While the sexes in their ardour and young life are thus captivated and absorbed, the arch enemy is employed in kindling raging fires in the soul, and infusing moral poison into the life-blood. The panorama vanishes—but these fires live, and perhaps it is not within the influence of ordinary grace to remove, in this life, the smouldering ashes, even where these raging fires may, by a divine power, have been extinguished. But in one, whose principles are not fixed, whose habits are unformed, they uproot the foundations, and sweep over all that is fair, with the desolating besom of destruction. Byron has the power to command the feelings of his readers in favour of his hero, and, make the moral distinctions we will, we wish that hero success. He is always made successful. But Byron's hero is a villain of the deepest dye, and here we are conducted to the true moral of his most fascinating pieces.

If the fire and energy of Byron's genius could have been exerted under the influence of that divine principle which warmed the heart of the "royal psalmist," instead of casting fire-brands into the citadel of civil, social, and domestic life, he might have kindled the altar of our sacrifice, and with a wing, I had almost said, such as ministering angels use, might have fanned the flame of our devotion. But shall we embrace the fallen angel, because he is an angel still? There is Watts, a heavenly muse. There is Cowper, whose lyre is touched by the gentle breezes of heaven, and pours angelic strains. There is Henry Kirke White, though a star in the distance, bright, mild and propitious. There are Milton, Pollock, Montgomery, Thomas Campbell, Wordsworth, Thomson, and Heber; and I may mention of your own sex, Hemans, Sigourney and Jane Taylor, worthy of your patronage, poetic, pure, evangelical. We need not go to the infernal regions for genius. It is found in the courts above. And while there are treasures of chaste and exalted literature untried and inexhaustible, I beg you to leave Byron, and Tom Moore, and even Pope, unexpurgated, to occupy the shelves of others, and to corrupt the morals of those, who are left to them.

## LETTER XL.

### PRACTICAL ADVICE.

MY DEAR CHILDREN,—As you are advancing to maturity, and now begin to mingle with mixed society, allow me to throw into a narrow compass some practical rules and maxims which you may find of great use, and the importance of which you will begin immediately to feel.

In the first place, I will say then, endeavour always to look at things as they are. Avoid visionary views. You will always have to do with the realities of life. All, therefore, which magnifies or diminishes things beyond reality, unfits the mind for safe and efficient action. Avoid, therefore, all prejudice, passion, strong party feeling, personal hatred, a spirit of envy, malice, or revenge, which always unfit the mind to judge soberly and truly. Every unnatural excitement produces this effect, and this may not only come of intemperance, but from any one of the sources just enumerated. In a state of excitement, things are made to appear different from what they really are, and if, under the illusion, you are not urged on to high crimes, you may do some indiscreet act, which will embitter life, and require to be repented of.

Never permit yourselves to be out of humour, especially with a dumb animal, or inanimate object. The brute acts from impulse or instinct, and when you act from passion, you put yourself on a level with him. Consider, too, that when you permit yourselves to be displeased with an inanimate object, you take a still bolder stand to act a more depraved part. You fight against Providence. Did you ever figure to yourselves Xerxes chastising the waves of the Hellespont? I have sometimes wondered that scene has never, among other objects, employed the pencil of the painter. How pigmy-like Xerxes would appear in the picture, giving, with feeble voice, command to the elements, amid the roar of the angry Bosphorus, lashing the shore and rolling its surges mountain high! How puny his uplifted arm applying the whip to chastise their insolence! How contemptible, throwing the chains, which are immediately swallowed up by the element that bids defiance to his threats and rage! Then to see him contending with the Almighty who rides on the whirlwind, and directs the storm, daring heaven to single combat! It is a subject which language imperfectly reaches, but I think it might be put upon canvass, and made to speak expressively.

Now what Xerxes was, in his rage against the sea, you may consider a young lady to be, on a smaller scale, when she loses her temper, or frets against Providence.

Realities are what we have to meet. To know them is truth. To perform our duties under the government of God in every relation to that truth is religion. Avoid high wrought and extravagant feelings on every subject, even on religious subjects, except as truth leads the way, and that will ever make you sober, deliberate, concerned with things as they are.

Speak always with candour and consideration. Indiscreet speech makes more work for repentance, with most persons, than overt and flagrant acts of error. It creates more wars than all other causes. It originates, probably, nine-tenths of all the personal conflicts which occur. I have sometimes thought that if I could regulate my speech to exact propriety, I could easily regulate every other part of conduct. It is very easy to say a thing. But once said, it can never be recalled,* and we usually feel that it must be maintained. Most persons talk too much. How rare a virtue is silence! Still more rare, the man or woman who never speaks inopportunely, and always speaks

* Semel emissum, volat irrevocabile verbum.—Hor.

"Our words are our own no longer than they remain unspoken."

what ought to be spoken. You know how it is in experience. "Miss B—— said so," and that starts the ball. Lazy as many may be in ordinary duties, here is all activity. There are enough volunteers to keep it in motion. It flies with accelerated velocity. And like a stone which the delicate touch of a single hand started from the top of a mountain, it soon acquires a force which no human power can resist. It bears down all in its way, and spreads desolation in its track. Be careful how you start these stones. While on the poise, they are in your power. Once moved, they soon become beyond control. So are words —little words. So may be a touch, a gentle touch, a pointing of the finger, or a cast of the eye. Such is the tongue among our members; such is our conversation in society. If you learn to govern the tongue, and regulate your speech, you gain a victory, and may avoid many conflicts.

Be especially careful not to report in one family what you have heard said in another; nor to one friend what may have been imprudently whispered to her disadvantage, except when truth and vital interests demand it. The tale bearer and informer is a mischief-maker, and although he may be listened to with earnestness, he cannot but be despised.

In your social relations, avoid a suspicious temper; yet presume on the friendship of no one.

Be always ready to grant all the favours you can, consistently with your duties to yourselves and others; but never do favours on the supposition that others are equally ready to reciprocate them. If you commence otherwise, you will be painfully taught that a warm heart bestows its charities on a cold world.

Be not too confiding. There is one inference which has done much injury. Because a man is regarded as a good man, it is therefore presumed that he will always do what is right. Let your own view of what is right be always higher authority than that of any mortal, whose opinion conflicts with your principles.

If a particular friend offers you special favours, use them not too liberally. If he puts a favourite article at your disposal, the strength of his friendship may prove to be weak should you practise too freely on his indulgence. When a friend that you wish to retain offers special favours, it is well for you if you are not obliged to use them.

Be indulgent toward the faults of others, severe towards your own. We are often impatient of the infirmities of others, forgetting that what in them offends us, may pertain, in a great degree, to ourselves. The same weak, and offensive, and erring natures pertain to all, and we are frail, feeble and offensive to others, wherein we often congratulate or excuse ourselves.

## LETTER XLI.

### PRACTICAL ADVICE.

My dear Children,—Industry is a duty expressly prescribed, and rendered necessary by our circumstances. A drone is offensive to nature, and worse than useless in society. The universal and necessary attendant of idleness is vice. Industry, therefore, should be formed to a habit. This done, like all other habits, it becomes a second nature.

Be industrious, whether engaged in study, domestic duties, or devotion. Life is short. The much we have to do will press heavily on the heels of our dying hour, and hurry us unprepared into eternity, unless we are diligent to accomplish the work which belongs to time. "The works of the righteous follow them." In an important sense, this is true of all, since we shall be judged according to our works. Let this fearful annunciation influence you to diligence in those works, whose results you will be willing to meet at the judgment day. To be busily employed is sometimes thought to be unworthy of a lady. I never desire to see you *such* ladies, nor *associated* with such. Aim to be something more than "playthings," and to do something more than play.

Let your labours be directed to some useful purpose. Some ladies act as if it were their "being's end and aim" to be busy about trifles, and to trifle with everything, to trifle with the other sex, with money, with time, with life, with death, with God and eternity. "Be ye not like unto them." Be not willing to come to the close of life with the world no better for your having lived in it. Make life productive of a good end, by doing good both to yourselves and others. Keep that end in view, and let every day advance you towards it.

> "Mark that day lost, whose low descending sun
> Views from your hand no worthy action done."

While you avoid idleness, take care, on the other hand, never to be in a hurry. Be deliberately diligent. "Haste makes waste." Do every thing with a calm and persevering temper. Those who never have any leisure often accomplish as little, and live to as little purpose, as others who live in idleness. Diligence in duty gains time, and gives us leisure to wait on our friends, or to relax in innocent amusement. I dislike to see a lady always so much engaged that she cannot see her friends. It is an affectation. Those who do their duties in proper time and order will find leisure for all social and relative duties.

You may easily gain leisure if you do earnestly what you do, do it at once, without delay, and withal do it well, that you may not need to do it again. Take time by the forelóck. If you delay till to-morrow what can be done to-day, it will be crowded into company with other duties and produce confusion. Then comes hurry, and consequent loss. Thus the duty may never be done at all, and how important soever it may be, you must meet the consequences. To defer present duty is to decide that you will not do your duty. What belongs to the present hour is duty. Delay it, and who can measure the consequences?

Finish whatever you undertake. Acquire the habit of completing your business. Then you will be prepared for the next, and there will be a consistency and adaptation of parts.

Should you leave your garments half finished, and throw them on in that imperfect state, how ridiculous would you appear before the public! Yet this is truly the attitude assumed by those persons who half perform their duties, and leave everything incomplete, except that the results are, in the last case, far the most serious and fatal. The first may expose us to present ridicule, but the other will subject us to lasting shame, "confusion and contempt."

Attempt great things. While you avoid visionary views, this rule will never be abused. In your sober senses, soberly employed, you will, of course, attempt what is practicable, and what is useful. You will not be disappointed. Diligence and perseverance in pursuit of practicable objects, will result in acquisition.

Never suffer discouragement. A single failure, or any failure, may not be final. Persevere.

> "The worst prognostic of the darkest day,
> Live till to-morrow, may have passed away."

If you do not succeed to your wishes, think little of it. Failure in ordinary objects is often better than success. If successful, avoid exultation. That is often worse in its effects than failure itself. A well balanced mind will go on in the performance of duty, as such. The results are of less importance than the duty. If we can never be happy but in success, and if nothing but success will satisfy us, we must be unhappy, for who is either always wise, or always successful? Our happiness can be made to depend safely on nothing but the performance of duty. Take a young lady at school, let her be diligent in study, ambitious, and persevering,—but let her suspend her happiness entirely on a given measure of success, on the attainment of particular honours, on the premiums awarded to the best, and how uncertain her victory; how frail the tenure of her happiness! If she fail to the end, she suffers the mortification of defeat after all the drudgery of her efforts. How different another, who has applied herself diligently to study as a duty, and been made happy all along in the performance of the duty itself! If she gains an honour, that is a contingent circumstance, adding to her sum of enjoyment, but not capable of destroying it, or of materially abridging it, though withheld.

Happiness is not a plant of earthly growth. It strikes its root by the "tree of life," and thrives in stinted measure amid the thorns and briers, which have sprung vigorously under the curse. Those who seek it here, seek for "perpetual sunshine mid perpetual storms." We shall find it only in heaven. Be satisfied, then, with what is practicable. Look at things as they are. Realize this is a world of trial. Be diligent in duty. Seek the satisfaction which will attend on a blameless life. Hope in God. Walk with him. Take up your cross. Bear it. Suffer under it. These trials will soon be over, and we shall meet each other—meet your little sister who has gone before—meet your dear mother—meet, a happy family in heaven.

www.ingramcontent.com/pod-product-compliance
Lightning Source LLC
LaVergne TN
LVHW050512100826
845148LV00002B/307

*9781425521646*